Study Guide

for

Essentials of American Government:
Continuity and Change,
2006 Edition

prepared by

John Ben Sutter

Houston Community College

New York Boston San Francisco
London Toronto Sydney Tokyo Singapore Madrid
Mexico City Munich Paris Cape Town Hong Kong Montreal

Study Guide for Essentials of American Government: Continuity and Change, 2006 Edition

Copyright ©2006 Pearson Education, Inc.

ISBN: 0-321-33785-9

2 3 4 5 6 7 8 9 10–OPM–08 07 06

TABLE OF CONTENTS

SECTION I

STUDY SKILLS

This section is designed to give you a number of ideas about how you can learn better study skills. Studying is an individual thing—what works for you might not work for others. So please use these hints to think about what tips you can use to improve your own skills.

If a suggestion doesn't work for you, try something else. But consciously think about how you study best, what kinds of settings work for you, what times of day help you to recall facts, and so on. Often, your study skills improve when you simply think consciously about how to study. If you need more help, see your professor, consult the suggested Web pages at the end of this section, and or find out what kind of help is available on campus. Most campuses today offer tutoring and counseling, often including classes on studying.

An overview of this section:

- **Note-taking**

- **Reading**

- **Taking Tests**
    - **Essay Tests**
    - **Objective Tests**

- **"The Ten Traps of Studying"**

- **Web Sites of Interest**

NOTE-TAKING

Good notes often make the difference between good and superior students. Bad note-taking often serves only to confuse. No one system works for everyone, but here are a number of rules of thumb that should be helpful as you devise your own system.

The main rule of note-taking is to do what you find helpful and comfortable. Often comparing your notes to those of your colleagues or asking you professor to look at one day's notes will help you determine how well you perform this task.

1) **GO TO CLASS!!!** The single easiest way—actually, the only way—to figure out what the professor will emphasize on a test, is to attend class daily. Missing class and getting the notes from someone else is a poor substitute for attendance. Besides, "repetition is the mother of learning," as the saying goes. And if you hear it AND write it, you will be more likely to remember it.

2) **Think about taking notes BEFORE you start.** In other words, have a plan. A common way of doing this is to draw a vertical line down the paper dividing it into two parts. Take notes to the right of the line. Save the left to add information that is given to you later, for your own thoughts on the subject and for notes about the information, as you study for tests later. An alternative is to use a spiral notebook (or similar style) and use the right-hand page for notes and the left-hand page for comments, etc. Or, use a loose leaf binder so you can sort your notes and add handouts. There are many ways to organize your notes.

3) **Sit up front!** This will help you concentrate (particularly in subjects that you do not find fascinating). You will also appear interested and excited to the professor; never a bad thing!

4) **Read and prepare for class IN ADVANCE!** It will be much easier to discern the important points in a lecture if you are already familiar with the material. You will also be able to answer questions asked in class. Plus, repetition is an excellent way to remember material. It also helps to review your notes from previous classes prior to each session. This will help you at exam time, and help you to reconnect with the material and see links among topics.

5) **Arrive early and stay for the whole class.** The first sentence or two uttered by the professor often tell you what the lecture will be about; the lecture will make less sense without the context. Also, a large amount of information is often given out in the last ten minutes of class as a professor strives to cover the material. If you are putting your stuff away and zipping your book bag, not only are you being rude and making obnoxious levels of noise, but you are missing important material.

6) **LISTEN closely to the lecture or discussion.** In particular try to pick out the following:

- Ideas and concepts
- Signal words: " in contrast," "on the other hand," "What I mean here is," "The important idea is," and so on
- If something is unclear, <u>ask a question</u>!

7) **Take Notes, not Dictation!** Your job is not to take down every word but to summarize the points and note the facts. Use indentation, underlining, highlighting, and/or outlining to get the important information down.

- Be brief, get main ideas down.
- Use your own words.
- Use symbols to emphasize important points, such as * or !
- Leave spaces for words and ideas you missed or that are covered out of sequence.

8) **You should always write down:**

- Names
- Dates and significant events
- Concepts, ideas, or phrases that are repeated
- Formulas, charts, drawings, etc. put on the board
- Examples given by the professor
- Professor's biases, if identifiable

9) **Find a way to make the subject interesting!** You won't remember what you consider boring and useless. You can make anything interesting with a positive attitude and a little creativity.

10) **Do not abbreviate unless** you will know later what the abbreviation stands for. Writing SC throughout your notes could mean social contract, Supreme Court, or South Carolina. Be consistent, whatever you choose. Standard abbreviations that might save you time include the following:

w/	=	with	Const	=	Constitution
w/o	=	without	dem	=	democracy
#	=	number	K	=	contract
vs	=	versus	pres	=	president
=	=	equals	nat'l	=	national
fed'l	=	federal			

11) **Review early and often!** Skim your lectures notes before each session of class. It is a good idea to review your notes immediately after class, while the information is still fresh, so you can correct mistakes and spell out problematic abbreviations, etc. Add to your notes. Jot down ideas you have had since class, how the information in one chapter relates to that of another chapter, compare your notes from class with your reading notes and integrate them. It is helpful to outline your notes and keep a list of definitions as you go. Both will make studying for tests easier.

READING

Yes, you are in college, so you know how to read. But how do you attack and comprehend boring or difficult material? Many students simply "get through" the reading assignment and then cannot answer questions in class and do not really understand the material. In order to read critically and analytically, you must be careful, thoughtful, and have a plan of attack before you dive in.

It is probably best that you do NOT use a highlighter. At least not in the way most students use them. Many students often color huge passages thoughtlessly as they read. This is not helpful in the long run. Don't highlight material in a chapter when you first open your textbook. In your first pass through the material, how do you know what's important and what's not? If you plunge right into the material, it, at first, might all seem important, and each page ends up entirely yellow from your highlighter! Set the highlighter down. Take time to consider what you're reading. Employ a style of **active reading.** This takes more time initially, but in the long run will save you time, because you will understand the material better, remember it longer, and be able to analyze what you have read.

Rules of Reading

- **Skim the chapter, book, or article first before you try to read it.** This provides you with a road map to the contents of the piece.

- **Use the guides provided by the author and publisher.** Tables of contents, appendices, tables of charts and graphs, glossaries, indices, etc. are there for you to use. They should help you get a handle on the material.

    - **Scan the table of contents.** Often textbooks provide more than one table of contents—an abbreviated one and a complete one.
    - **Read the preface!** In the preface, the author (or some other expert) tells you what they want you to get out of their book or why they wrote it.
    - **Examine the material in BOLD in the chapter:** Look at the chapter subheadings, the terms in the outside margins; examine the pictures and what's printed underneath them.

- **Use the end pieces:** appendices, indices, glossaries, etc.

- **Decide what you think you will learn from the work.** Think about what you are about to read. What questions do you have? Do you think the author has a bias? If so, what bias and why do you think there is one? Why did the professor assign this reading? What does he/she expect you to get out of it? Here, it is often helpful to look at your syllabus; the topic may give you some understanding of why this piece was assigned.

- **Read the piece fairly quickly** to get more information about main ideas and intent. Mark any passages that look particularly difficult. Circle unfamiliar words and phrases.

- **Now you are ready to really read the piece.**

  - **Take a notebook and a pen** and keep notes as you read. Write an outline on paper and use marginal notes in the book to argue with (or sometimes agree with) the author.
  - Never read for more than an hour without a break; if your eyes glaze over and you start to fall asleep, stop and **take a break.** (This means you cannot do your reading immediately prior to class—you need to plan ahead.)
  - At the end of each section or subsection, **stop and ask yourself what you just read.** Does it make sense? What were the main ideas? Any definitions you may need to know on a test? If you can't answer those questions, you need to reread the passages with more concentration.
  - At the end of the whole piece, you should be able to **identify the author's main points.** If not, you need to reread the piece or, if you took good reading notes, reviewing your notes should be sufficient.
  - Keep a good collegiate dictionary handy whenever you're reading. If you come across a word you don't understand, **look it up!** If you don't know what that word means, you might miss the meaning of the entire sentence, or even the entire section. (And never pass up a chance to broaden your vocabulary; words are your tools in your effort to communicate your ideas effectively to others.)

- Most texts offer **summaries and questions** at the end of a chapter or in a study guide such as this one. Use them to ensure your understanding of the material. You should be able to answer the questions posed and be able to flesh out the information provided in a summary. If not, again that is a signal that you need to review the material again.

- The best way to know you have mastered the material is to try to explain it to someone else. Think of this as a self-test. Discuss the material with your classmates, tell your roommate or spouse or friend about it, or make your family listen to your summaries.

TAKING TESTS

ALWAYS

- **Read or go over the entire test** before beginning to answer questions. You could quickly read through the whole essay exam, but don't try to read over an entire ten-page multiple choice exam. You should go over it so you know what to expect. If it is a multi-page exam and is mostly multiple choice but has an essay buried at the end, you're in trouble if you find that out 5 minutes before the end of class!

- **Make choices** if they are offered. In a multi-choice exam, eliminate the answers you know are right so that you can make a choice between fewer options.

- **Allot your time** carefully and **be aware of time during the test,** but do not set watch alarms; they will disturb others. If a question is worth 20 percent, you should spend only 20 percent of your time on it.

- Depending on your style and level of test anxiety, **choose the order** in which you will address the questions. Answer the easiest question first if you need a confidence builder, or answer the most difficult if you need to get it out of the way while you are fresh.

- **Be neat and legible.** If you are answering an objective-style exam on a Scantron, be sure to use a number two pencil and have a good, clean eraser. If you make an error, erase the incorrect mark cleanly and completely or you might lose points because of a mechanical grading error!

- **Ask questions** if you are unclear about content or procedure.

- Save time to **proofread and double check** your answers at the end.

HINTS for Essay Exams

1) **TIME**

The most challenging part of taking essay exams is often the management of time during the exam. This is extremely important, especially for those of you who often have trouble finishing an exam. Exams are more than just tests of knowledge. They teach and reinforce important lessons about discipline, organization, and your ability to communicate what you know. Exams place a premium on your ability to make up your mind about issues and concepts, as well as to organize your thoughts and write <u>concisely</u> and <u>lucidly</u> (clearly) about topics within a given time period.

> *Hint 1*: Start with the questions that are ***worth the most points***. Then if you run out of time, you can quickly jot down identifications and short answers. You cannot write an essay in five minutes!
>
> *Hint 2*: ***Organize and think before you start to write***, preferably before you come to class to take the exam. You should study by thinking of possible questions so that you are half-way there while still studying. This will save you time during the exam period.

2) CLARITY

Clarity is essential to earning a good grade on an essay. It is not enough to simply jot down all of the facts you have studied. You must address the question as asked. For example, if the question says to address the impact of the Anti-Federalists on the U.S. government, do not include a discussion of Congressional committees. You don't get points for writing a great essay if it doesn't answer the question your professor asks!

A competent exam answer will be clear and well-organized. You must have a point or an argument, as well as convey the facts.

> *Hint 3*: Be sure you ***know what the question means*** before you start writing!
>
> *Hint 4*: Use an outline to ***organize*** your thoughts before writing.
>
> *Hint 5*: Pay attention to ***keywords*** within the question and use them to understand the question and formulate the answer. For example:
>> Analyze
>> Compare and contrast
>> Discuss
>
> *Hint 6*: Keep your ***focus;*** don't wander off the subject.
>
> *Hint 7*: Read and respond to ***all parts*** of the question. Often students neglect to answer part of a question.

3) LANGUAGE

A good exam must be legible and readable in terms of grammar, punctuation and style as well as content. If your grammar and syntax are too convoluted, your meaning will be hopelessly obscured.

> *Hint 8*: Do not use words you can not define, and be sure to define all concepts you use. For example, if the question asks you to discuss the nature of federalism, ALWAYS begin with a **definition** and discussion of what that word means.
>
> *Hint 9*: Keep your sentences simple and your ideas will come through more clearly.

Hint 10: Avoid symbols and abbreviations. The professor may not be able to decipher them.

Hint 11: Do not use slang or colloquialisms. Do not write as you speak. An essay or essay exam is a **formal** means of conveying information.

Hint 12: **Organize!** Use paragraphs and essay format to make your essay clear and understandable. Start at the beginning and end at the end; do not jump around. If you are confused, your answer will be confused, and your grade will reflect that confusion!

4)   **CONTENT**

The single most important part of any exam is the content. You must have facts, theories, and a basic understanding of the material to do well.

Hint 13: Always choose to answer the questions you know best if a choice is given on an exam. Do not just answer the questions in order!

Hint 14: **Be specific and precise.** For example, if you are asked to identify Lyndon Johnson, do not simply say he was a President of the U.S. There have been many presidents. What did he do that was important? Why do we study him? When did he serve and how well did he govern? What is he famous for? In other words, why is your professor asking about this particular president? Answer the question given you specifically and precisely.

Hint 15: Be concise but not too concise. In other words, clarity and brevity are good, but do not overdo it and leave out important information.

Hint 16: **Do not assume** that the professor knows anything! This is your opportunity to demonstrate that YOU know it. Too often students tell their professor, "Well, I didn't include that because you already know that." You need to show your professor that YOU know it.

Hints for Objective Tests

1)   **Reconnoiter the test.** Briefly look over the entire test. Read the directions carefully. How long is it? Are there sections worth different amounts of points? Plan your strategy and allot your time.

2)   **Read each item carefully.** Don't lose points because you didn't notice a "not" or an "except" in the question. Always read every possibility. Even if answer choice (a) seems to be the most logical response, it may not be.

3)   **Answer only the questions you know cold on your first run through.** This will help you warm up and may jar your memory on tougher questions. It will also reduce your test anxiety and build your confidence.

4)   **Do not read too much into or out-think the question.** Most professors are not trying to trick you; they simply want to find out how much you have learned.

5) **Answer every question** unless there is a severe penalty for guessing. And when guessing, use some common sense. Things are rarely "always" or "never." If you can choose only one answer and two are virtually identical, you can probably rule out those two.

6) Always proofread and check your work. But **be careful about changing your first response** unless you are absolutely sure. First instincts are often correct.

"THE TEN TRAPS OF STUDYING"

reproduced with the permission of the Counseling and Psychological Services of the University of North Carolina, Chapel Hill

1. "I Don't Know Where To Begin"

Take Control. Make a list of all the things you have to do. Break your workload down into manageable chunks. Prioritize! Schedule your time realistically. Don't skip classes near an exam—you may miss a review session. Use that hour in between classes to review notes. Interrupt study time with planned study breaks. Begin studying early, with an hour or two per day, and slowly build as the exam approaches.

2. "I've Got So Much To Study…And So Little Time"

Preview. Survey your syllabus, reading material, and notes. Identify the most important topics emphasized and areas still not understood. Previewing saves time, especially with nonfiction reading, by helping you organize and focus on the main topics. Adapt this method to your own style and study material, but remember, previewing is not an effective substitute for reading.

3. "This Stuff Is So Dry, I Can't Even Stay Awake Reading It"

Attack! Get actively involved with the text as you read. Ask yourself, "What is important to remember about this section?" Take notes or underline key concepts. Discuss the material with others in your class. Study together. Stay on the offensive, especially with material that you don't find interesting, rather than reading passively and missing important points.

4. "I Read It. I Understand It. But I Just Can't Get It To Sink In"

Elaborate. We remember best the things that are most meaningful to us. As you are reading, try to elaborate upon new information with your own examples. Try to integrate what you're studying with what you already know. You will be able to remember new material better if you can link it to something that's already meaningful to you. Some techniques include:

Chunking: An effective way to simplify and make information more meaningful. For example, if you wanted to remember the colors in the visible spectrum (Red, Orange, Yellow, Green, Blue, Indigo, Violet), you would have to memorize seven "chunks" of information in order. But when you take the first letter of each color and spell the name "Roy G. Biv," you reduce the information to three "chunks."

Mnemonics: Any memory-assisting technique that helps us to associate new information with something familiar. For example, to remember a formula or equation, we may use letters of the alphabet to represent certain numbers. Then we can change an abstract formula into a more meaningful word or phrase, so we'll be able to remember it better. Sound-alike associations can be very effective, too, especially while trying to learn a new language. The key is to create your own links, so you won't forget them.

5.   "I Guess I Understand It"

Test yourself. Make up questions about key sections in notes or reading. Keep in mind what the professor has stressed in the course. Examine the relationships between concepts and sections. Often, simply by changing section headings you can generate many effective questions. For example, a section entitled "Bystander Apathy" might be changed into questions such as: "What is bystander apathy?" "What are the causes of bystander apathy?" and "What are some examples of bystander apathy?"

6.   "There's Too Much To Remember"

Organize. Information is recalled better if it is represented in an organized framework that will make retrieval more systematic. There are many techniques that can help you organize new information, including: Write chapter outlines or summaries; emphasize relationships between sections. Group information into categories or hierarchies where possible.

Information Mapping. Draw up a matrix to organize and interrelate material. For example, if you were trying to understand the causes of World War I, you could make a chart listing all the major countries involved across the top, and then list the important issues and events down the side. Next, in the boxes in between, you could describe the impact each issue had on each country to help you understand these complex historical developments.

7.   "I Knew It A Minute Ago"

Review. After reading a section, try to recall the information contained in it. Try answering the questions you made up for that section. If you cannot recall enough, re-read portions you had trouble remembering. The more time you spend studying, the more you tend to recall. Even after the point where information can be perfectly recalled, further study makes the material less likely to be forgotten entirely. In other words, you can't over-study. However, how you organize and integrate new information is still more important than how much time you spend studying.

8.   **"But I Like To Study In Bed"**

Context. Recall is better when study contexts (physical location, as well as mental, emotional, and physical state) are similar to the test context. The greater the similarity between the study setting and the test setting, the greater the likelihood that material studied will be recalled during the test.

9.   **"Cramming Before A Test Helps Keep It Fresh In My Mind"**

Spacing. Start studying now. Keep studying as you go along. Begin with an hour or two a day about one week before the exam, and then increase study time as the exam approaches. Recall increases as study time gets spread out over time.

10.   **"I'm Gonna Stay Up All Night 'til I Get This"**

Avoid Mental Exhaustion. Take short breaks often when studying. Before a test, have a rested mind. When you take a study break, and just before you go to sleep at night, don't think about academics. Relax and unwind, mentally and physically. Otherwise, your break won't refresh you and you'll find yourself lying awake at night. It's more important than ever to take care of yourself before an exam! Eat well, sleep, and get enough exercise.

WEB SITES OF INTEREST

These are simply starting points. There are many free and quite a few commercial sites on the Internet devoted to learning, study skills, etc. A little surfing will yield many more. And remember, the more conscious you are about your coursework and studying, the better you are likely to do.

Some College and University Web Pages on Study Skills:

Middle Tennessee State University offers strategies for success in college from note-taking to memory and learning styles.
        www.mtsu.edu/~studskl

The **University of North Carolina** Web site offers "Study Habits and the Ten Traps of Studying" plus more on skills and success in college.

http://caps.unc.edu/TenTraps.html

Southern Illinois University offers study help online as well as numerous links to other sites with similar goals.
http://www.siu.edu/departments/cola/psycho/intro/studying.html

Virginia Tech's Division of Student Affairs offers many tips for studying, reading, taking notes, etc.
http://www.ucc.vt.edu/stdyhlp.html

Dallas County Community Colleges hosts a Web site with numerous links to study aids in a number of areas, categorized for easy reference.
http://ollie.dcccd.edu/Services/StudyHelp/StudySkills

SECTION II

This section of the study guide will help you study each chapter of the O'Connor text. Each chapter is broken down into several parts, to help you understand and remember the material:

- **Chapter Goals and Learning Objectives**

- **Chapter Outlines and Key Points**

- **Research Ideas and Possible Paper Topics**

- **Web Sites**

- **Practice Tests**
  - **Multiple Choice**
  - **True/False**
  - **Compare and Contrast**
  - **Essay and Short Answer Questions**

CHAPTER 1
THE POLITICAL LANDSCAPE

Chapter Goals and Learning Objectives

To understand the present, one must understand history, particularly with regard to who we are as a nation. Where did we come from? What were and are our goals? Why does our government look, act, and function the way that it does? Equipped with such understanding, we can be better citizens and, in turn, make government better. This nation is changing, as it always has. Americans are not satisfied with the workings of government, and many do not understand how the government is supposed to work. We believe that a thorough understanding of the system, how it works, and why we are not satisfied, are essential to improving and reforming the system, so that it works better and we are more satisfied with it. We hope that this understanding helps you become a better informed and more active participant in the political process. According to President Harry S. Truman, "In order to be a good citizen, you must know your country's history."

This chapter is designed to give you an overview of the subject of the text, as well as a look at the theories and ideas that underpin our political and economic system. The main topic headings of the chapter are:

- The Political Landscape
- Government: What It Is and Why We Need It
- Roots of American Government: Where Did the Ideas Come From?
- American Political Culture and the Characteristics of American Democracy
- Changing Characteristics of the American People
- Ideology of the American Public
- Current Attitudes Toward American Government

In each section, there are certain facts and ideas that you should strive to understand. Many are in boldface type and appear in both the narrative and in the glossary at the end of the book. Other ideas, dates, facts, events, people, etc. are more difficult to pull out of the narrative. (Keep in mind that studying for objective-style tests [multiple choice, T/F] is different than studying for essay tests. See the Study Guide section on test taking for hints on study skills.)

In general, after you finish reading and studying this chapter, you should understand the following:

- What government is and why we need it
- The roots of American government
- American political culture and democracy
- The changing characteristics of the American people
- Political ideologies of the American public

- The current attitudes Americans have toward government and the role it plays in their lives

---

Chapter Outline and Key Points

In this section, you are provided with a basic outline of the chapter and key words/points you should know. Use this outline to develop a complete outline of the material. Write the definitions or further explanations for the terms. Use the space provided in this workbook or rewrite that material in your notebook. This will help you study and remember the material in preparation for your tests, assignments, and papers.

The Political Landscape

meaning of phrase "We the people"—

America as the world's "best hope"—

Government: What It is and Why We Need It

government—

citizen—

politics—

Functions of Government

Framers' belief of what the major function of government was—

establishing justice—

ensuring domestic tranquility—

providing for the common defense—

promoting the general welfare—

securing the blessings of liberty—

Roots of American Government: Where Did the Ideas Come From?

Types of Government

monarchy—

totalitarianism—

oligarchy—

democracy—

The Reformation and the Enlightenment: Questioning the Divine Right of Kings

Enlightenment—

divine right of kings—

the Pilgrims—

social contract—

Hobbes, Locke, and a Social Contract Theory of Government

social contract theory—

Thomas Hobbes—

Leviathan (1651)—

John Locke—

natural rights—

life, liberty, and property—

Thomas Jefferson and the original draft of the Declaration of Independence—

Devising a National Government in the American Colonies

what the colonists rejected and were fearful of—

direct democracy—

indirect democracy (representative democracy)—

republic—

American Political Culture and the Characteristics of American Democracy

political culture—

Personal Liberty

personal liberty—

Fourteenth Amendment—

Equality

political equality—

Popular Consent and Majority Rule

popular consent—

majority rule—

Bill of Rights—

Popular Sovereignty—

popular sovereignty—

natural law—

Building Civil Society

civil society—

Individualism

individualism—

Jefferson's statement on individualism in the Declaration of Independence—

Changing Characteristics of the American People

Changing Size and Population

U.S. population today and when Constitution adopted—

U.S. Population, 1790-2050 (Figure 1.2)—

population and representation in Congress—

Changing Demographics of the U.S. Population

aging of America—

Changes in Racial and Ethnic Composition—
　　　Race and Ethnicity in America: 2000 and Beyond (Figure 1.3)—

Changes in Age Cohort Composition—

　　　Baby Boomers—

　　　Generation X—

　　　Generation Y—

Changes in Family and Family Size—

　　　effect of birth control and industrialization—

　　　why couples began to limit the size of their families—

　　　change from "traditional" family households—

Implications of These Changes

Ideology of the American Public

political ideology—

Conservatives—

Liberals—

Libertarians—

Problems with Political Labels

chart your views on political ideology (Table 1.2)—

self-identification as to political ideology, 1974-2002 (Figure 1.4)—

Current Attitudes Toward American Government

American Dream—

four major networks—

expansion of alternatives to network news—

High Expectations

growth of federal government—

role of state government in everyday lives of Americans—

A Missing Appreciation of the Good

faith in American institutions (Table 1.3)—

how Americans are really doing (Table 1.4)—

Mistrust of Politicians

why there is such mistrust of politicians—

Voter Apathy

reasons Americans do not vote—

Redefining Our Expectations

Research Ideas and Possible Paper Topics

1) Discuss how and why the interpretation of the phrase "We the People" has changed so dramatically over the last 200 plus years.

2) How will the Internet change American political culture? Will it be more or less democratic? Discuss the effects the Internet is having on politics and will have in the future.

3) Compare and contrast the economic systems of socialism, communism, totalitarianism, and capitalism.

4) Discuss the nature of the challenges to America posed by the changing racial, ethnic, and age distribution in society. Look at historical precedents as well as more philosophical arguments.

5)   What are some of the reasons voters give for not going to the polls, and how can voter turnout in the United States be improved?

Web Sites

U.S. Census Bureau offers information on the demographic, geographic, and economic make-up of our country. Includes the ability to search for state-level data.
        http://www.census.gov

The University of Michigan Documents Center page titled "Statistical Resources on the Web for Political Science" provides a one-stop academic research site for students, listing numerous links to sites to assist in researching political, racial, ethnic, social, and other demographic information.
        http://www.lib.umich.edu/govdocs/stpolisc.html

The **Gallup Organization** offers up-to-date and historical perspectives on the opinions of the American public.
        www.gallup.com

Brandeis University's Political Philosophy Internet Resources Web page provides links to numerous sites of interest in political philosophy.
        http://people.brandeis.edu/~teuber/polphil.html

To better understand the Enlightenment, go to a marvelous Web site developed by a high school history teacher in Mesquite, Texas titled **TeacherOz.com**. The Enlightenment page lists scores of resources. (The TeacherOz.com Web site received a recommendation by The History Channel.)
        www.teacheroz.com/Enlightenment.htm

Yahoo.com. Yahoo is a commercial search engine that has a wide variety of information. For our purposes, there is a government subheading of Yahoo that will provide you with links to many topics on government, regime type, ideology, political thought, and more.
        www.yahoo.com/government

Practice Tests

MULTIPLE CHOICE

1)   The type of government where the rule of one in the interest of all, a government rejected by the Framers of the Constitution, is called a
        a.   monarchy.
        b.   totalitarian state.

c. oligarchy.

d. democracy.

2) The first political philosopher to argue the necessity of government to control society because of mankind's bestial tendencies, and that without government life would be "solitary, poor, nasty, brutish and short," was

a. John Locke.

b. Thomas Hobbes.

c. Baron de Montesquieu.

d. Jean Jacques Rousseau.

3) The idea that men form governments largely to preserve life, liberty, and property comes from

a. John Locke.

b. Thomas Hobbes.

c. Baron de Montesquieu.

d. Jean Jacques Rousseau.

4) In the original draft of the Declaration of Independence, Thomas Jefferson directly quoted which Enlightenment philosopher with regard to rights?

a. John Locke

b. Thomas Hobbes

c. Baron de Montesquieu

d. Jean Jacques Rousseau

5) The belief that all people are free and equal by natural right and that this requires that a government which rules the people be one of the consent of those governed is called

a. a monarchy.

b. political culture.

c. an oligarchy.

d. social contract theory.

6) A system of government in which representatives of the people are chosen by ballot is called

a. hegemonic democracy.

b. tutelary democracy.

c. indirect democracy.

d. direct democracy.

7) The set of attitudes, beliefs, and values that people have toward how their government should operate is called

a. public opinion.

b. norms.

c. ideology.

d. political culture.

8)   The idea of popular sovereignty, the right of a people to govern themselves, has its basis in
    a.   Greek mythology.
    b.   the writings of Thomas Hobbes.
    c.   natural law.
    d.   empirical theory.

9)   The population of the United States around the time of the ratification of the Constitution was
    a.   1 million.
    b.   4 million.
    c.   30 million.
    d.   100 million.

10)   For the first time, the U.S. population is getting
    a.   younger.
    b.   older.
    c.   shorter.
    d.   thinner.

11)   An individual's coherent set of values and beliefs about the purpose and scope of government are called
    a.   individualism.
    b.   attitude.
    c.   political culture.
    d.   political ideology.

12)   One who favors a free market and no governmental interference in personal and economic affairs is called a
    a.   libertarian.
    b.   conservative.
    c.   liberal.
    d.   mercantilist.

13)   One who favors governmental regulation of the economy to protect the environment and the rights of workers, and who stresses the need for social services to aid the poor, is called a
    a.   libertarian.
    b.   conservative.
    c.   liberal.
    d.   mercantilist.

14)   "During the first 150 years of our nations' history, which government was more powerful in matters affecting the everyday lives of Americans?"

a. state governments
b. the federal government
c. the United Nations
d. the North Atlantic Treaty Organization

15) Many Americans don't vote because they
a. have no time.
b. lack enough information on the issues and candidates.
c. are content.
d. All of the above.

TRUE/FALSE

1) "We the people" are the first three words of the Declaration of Independence.

2) In an oligarchy, power rests in the hands of the people, either through elected representatives or directly.

3) The Reformation and the Enlightenment altered the nature of government as people began to believe they could also have a say in their own governance.

4) Thomas Hobbes argued that man's natural state was war, and government was necessary to restrain man's bestial tendencies.

5) The American system tries to balance the ideals of majority rule and minority rights.

6) Since 1970, the number of female-headed households in the United States has decreased dramatically.

7) Liberals favor local and state action over federal action and emphasizes less government regulation of the economy.

8) A libertarian is someone who favors an unfettered free market with no governmental interference in personal liberties.

9) Studies show that many Americans who label themselves conservative actually take fairly liberal positions on social issues.

10) American voters, unlike voters in most other societies, get a chance to vote for a host of candidates and issues.

COMPARE AND CONTRAST

natural law and social contract theory

the theories of Thomas Hobbes and John Locke

direct democracy and indirect democracy

majority rule and minority rights

elite theory, interest group theory, bureaucratic theory, and pluralist theory

conservatism, libertarianism, and liberalism

ESSAY AND SHORT ANSWER QUESTIONS

1) The Preamble to the U.S. Constitution introduces the document that has guided our nation since 1789. What does it say, and why is it important?

2) What is popular consent, and what are its historical origins?

3) What impact has, and will, the Internet have on our democracy and system of government?

4) What is political culture in general, and what is American political culture?

5) Discuss the origins of the American government. (Hint: What philosophies guided the American colonists as they created a new system of government?)

6) What are the characteristics of American democracy?

7) In order to understand the nature of the American government, one must know who the American people are. Discuss the demographics of the United States and their effects on the political system.

8) Many Americans seem displeased with their government and politicians. Discuss whether this is the case and why.

9) What are the problems with political labels?

10) Discuss some current attitudes of Americans toward their government.

ANSWERS TO STUDY EXERCISES

multiple choice answers

1.	a	p. 6
2.	b	p. 8
3.	a	p. 8
4.	a	p. 8
5.	d	p. 7, 8
6.	c	p. 9
7.	d	p. 9
8.	c	p. 10
9.	b	p. 12
10.	b	p. 13
11.	d	p. 20
12.	a	p. 21
13.	c	p. 21
14.	a	p. 23
15.	d	p. 24, 25

true/false answers

1.	F	p. 1
2.	F	p. 6
3.	T	p. 7
4.	T	p. 7
5.	T	p. 10
6.	T	p. 18
7.	F	p. 21
8.	T	p. 21
9.	T	p. 21
10.	T	p. 24

CHAPTER 2
THE CONSTITUTION

Chapter Goals and Learning Objectives

To better understand the nature of a constitution, let us examine the importance of a foundation to a building. To build a house or some such structure you first must lay a foundation. The foundation buttresses the structure, gives it support and definition. You build your house directly atop the foundation. Anything not built on that foundation surely will fall from lack of definition and support.

The foundation of our system of government is the Constitution. Our nation and its laws are built upon it. The U.S. Constitution is one of the longest-lasting and least-amended constitutions in the world and has endured despite changing demographics, changing technology, and changing ideas. The problems encountered and compromises made by the Framers of the Constitution continue to affect our nation and our political process. Yet, the structure created and supported by our Constitution still stands. It is important to understand why. An understanding of the Constitutional era is essential to understanding our political system.

This chapter is designed to give you a basic understanding of the colonial era and the events that led to the writing of the Declaration of Independence, the main grievances of the colonists against the Crown and Parliament, the first American government under the Articles of Confederation, the writing of the Constitution, the nature of the U.S. Constitution, and the ratification debate.

The main topic headings of the chapter are:

- The Origins of a New Nation
- The Declaration of Independence
- The First Attempt at Government: The Articles of Confederation
- The Miracle at Philadelphia: Writing a Constitution
- The U.S. Constitution
- The Drive for Ratification
- Formal Methods of Amending the Constitution

In each section, there are certain facts and ideas that you should strive to understand. Many are in boldface type and appear in both the narrative and in the glossary at the end of the book. Other ideas, dates, facts, events, people, etc. are more difficult to pull out of the narrative. (Keep in mind that studying for objective-style tests [multiple choice, T/F] is different than studying for essay tests. See the Study Guide section on test taking for hints on study skills.)

In general, after you finish reading and studying this chapter, you should understand the following:

- Why colonists came to the New World
- The nature of the American colonies under British rule and how they changed
- The break with Great Britain and the circumstances surrounding the eruption of the Revolutionary War
- The Declaration of Independence and its philosophical underpinnings
- The first American government under the Articles of Confederation and the failings of that document
- The Constitutional Convention—who was there, what they did, why they did it
- The United States Constitution and what it says
- The controversy over ratification and the ratification debates between the Federalists and Anti-Federalists
- The Bill of Rights and the process for amending the Constitution

Chapter Outline and Key Points

In this section, you are provided with a basic outline of the chapter and key words/points you should know. Use this outline to develop a complete outline of the material. Write the definitions or further explanations for the terms. Use the space provided in this workbook or rewrite that material in your notebook. This will help you study and remember the material in preparation for your tests, assignments, and papers.

The Origins of a New Nation

oppressive British traditions absent in the New World—

Trade and Taxation

mercantilism—

French and Indian War—

Sugar Act—

Stamp Act—

Samuel Adams, Patrick Henry and the Sons of Liberty—

First Steps Toward Independence

Stamp Act Congress—

Townshend Acts—

Boston Massacre—

tea tax—

tea parties—

Coercive Acts (Intolerable Acts)—

The First Continental Congress

Committees of Correspondence—

First Continental Congress—

Second Continental Congress—

<u>The Declaration of Independence</u>

Thomas Pain and *Common Sense*—

first colony to call for independence—

confederation—

Declaration of Independence—

Thomas Jefferson—

John Locke and the Declaration of Independence—

<u>The First Attempts at Government: Articles of Confederation</u>

Articles of Confederation—

a confederation derives all its powers from the states—

Key provisions of the Articles of Confederation—

1)

2)

3)

4)

5)

Problems Under the Articles of Confederation—
Daniel Shays—

weaknesses of the Articles of Confederation:

1)

2)

3)

4)

5)

6)

7)

8)

9)

the greatest weakness of the Articles of Confederation—

The Miracle at Philadelphia: Writing a Constitution

Constitutional Convention of 1787—

The Virginia and New Jersey Plans

Virginia Plan—

New Jersey Plan—

Constitutional Compromises

Great Compromise—

Three-Fifths Compromise—

Unfinished Business Affecting the Executive Branch

recommendations of the Committee on Unfinished Portions—

Electoral College—

provision for removal of the chief executive—

<u>**The U.S. Constitution**</u>

Constitution—

The Preamble—

"We the People"—

The Basic Principles of the Constitution

Montesquieu—

major features of the Articles of Confederation and the Constitution (Table 2.1)—

federal system—

separation of powers—

judicial review—

checks and balances—

illustration of separation of power and checks and balances (Figure 2.1)—

The Articles of the Constitution

first three articles establish the three branches of government—

Article I: The Legislative Branch

legislative powers—

what the bicameral legislatures consists of—

enumerated powers—

necessary and proper clause (elastic clause)—

implied powers—

Article II: The Executive Branch

executive power—

president—

important powers of the president in section 3—

State of the Union Address—

Article III: The Judicial Branch

Supreme Court—

appointments for life—

Articles IV through VII

full faith and credit clause—

how amendments can be added to the Constitution—

supremacy clause—

no religious test for public office—

procedure for ratification of the new Constitution—

The Characteristics and Motives of the Framers

"Founding Fathers"—

Charles A. Beard and *An Economic Interpretation of the Constitution of the United States*—

Who Were the Framers? (p. 48)—

<u>The Drive for Ratification</u>

Federalists Versus Anti-Federalists

Federalists—

Anti-Federalists—

The Federalist Papers

"Publius"—

Hamilton, Madison, and Jay—

The Federalist Papers—

"Brutus" and "Cato"—

Anti-Federalist arguments—

Federalist No. 10 and 51—

Ratifying the Constitution

Article VII—

efforts of Hamilton and Madison—

Adding a Bill of Rights

A Student's Revenge: Twenty-Seventh [Madison] Amendment—

Bill of Rights—

Bill of Rights sought by the Anti-Federalists—

protections and guarantees of the Bill of Rights (Table 2.3)—

<u>**Formal Methods of Amending the Constitution**</u>

Formal Methods of Amending the Constitution

Article V—

two-stage amendment process—

two methods of proposal—

ratification—

ERA—

Informal Methods of Amending the Constitution

Judicial Interpretation

Marbury v. *Madison* (1803)—

criticisms of judicial review—

Social and Cultural Change

Great Depression and the New Deal—

Marriage Amendment—

advances in technology—

September 11, 2001—

Research Ideas and Possible Paper Topics

1) Read the Articles of Confederation and pose an argument that they were not flawed and should have been maintained as the American form of government.

2) Read some of the Federalist and Anti-Federalist Papers on a single topic: strength of the national government, nature of the executive, nature of the legislature, need for a strong defense, or other topic. Present each argument in a paper and then using the Papers as evidence, discuss your own views on the subject.

3) The text gives a few examples of how the Constitution has changed due to interpretations by the judiciary and others. Think about other ways in which the Constitution has changed or will soon change and write a paper.

4) One of the major factors in the reelection of George W. Bush as president in 2004 was the issue of same-sex marriages. Social conservatives pushed the president to announce his support of a constitutional amendment banning same-sex marriages. Why do they believe it is necessary to amend the Constitution to achieve the goal of prohibiting same-sex marriages? Put another way, what is one of the constitutional arguments made by proponents of same-sex marriages that contends the Constitution forbids the federal and state governments from banning same-sex marriages?

Cornell University site offers the complete text of the Constitution. Many terms are hyperlinked and cross-referenced to other key issues.
www.law.cornell.edu/constitution/constitution.table.html

The U.S. Constitution OnLine offers many documents, including the Articles of Confederation, Declaration of Independence, the Constitution, and many other links.
www.usconstitution.net

Kingwood College Library offers links to constitutions of the world.
www.nhmccd.cc.tx.us/contracts/lrc/kc/constitutions-subject.html

Search and download the text of the **Federalist Papers** from **The Avelon Project at Yale Law School**.
http://www.yale.edu/lawweb/avalon/federal/fed.htm

Turn to **GradeSaver's Classic Notes** for background on Alexander Hamilton, James Madison, and John Jay, as well as summaries and analysis of *The Federalist Papers*.
http://www.gradesaver.com/ClassicNotes/Titles/federalist/

The **Manuscript Division of the Library of Congress** offers a wide variety of documents from the fifteenth to twentieth centuries on American history.
http://lcweb2.loc.gov/ammem/mcchtml/corhome.html

National Museum of American History offers timelines, virtual exhibits, music, and other information from American history.
www.americanhistory.si.edu/

The University of Missouri-Kansas City hosts a Web site examining constitutional conflicts including the right to marry.
http://www.law.umkc.edu/faculty/projects/ftrials/conlaw/righttomarry.htm

Practice Tests

MULTIPLE CHOICE

1) The economic theory designed to increase a nation's wealth through developing commercial industry and a favorable balance of trade is called
   a. federalism.
   b. confederation.
   c. conservatism.
   d. mercantilism.

2) The first official meeting of the colonies and the first step toward a unified nation was/were the
   a. Stamp Act Congress.
   b. First Continental Congress.
   c. Committees of Correspondence.
   d. Colonial Parliament.

3) The type of government in which the national government derives its powers from independent member states is called
   a. shared sovereignty.
   b. unitary government.
   c. a confederation.
   d. federalism.

4) The Articles of Confederation failed due to a number of weaknesses, including that the national government
   a. could not regulate commerce among the states.
   b. could not tax its citizens or the states.
   c. lacked a strong central government.
   d. All of the above.

5) The proposal that first called for a bicameral legislature at the Constitutional Convention was called the
   a. New Jersey Plan.
   b. Virginia Plan.
   c. New York Plan.
   d. Great Compromise.

6) In general, at the Constitutional Convention, most of the small states felt comfortable with
   a. a stronger central government to deal with the crisis at hand.
   b. a concentration of power into a single branch of government.
   c. a unicameral legislature appointed by the president.
   d. the Articles of Confederation.

7) Reflecting the attitude of many of the Framers of the Constitution, including Alexander Hamilton, the election of the president of the United States would be removed from the hands of the "masses" through the creation of
   a. a bicameral legislature.
   b. the Senate, which would be elected by the states' legislatures.
   c. the Committee on Unfinished Portions.
   d. the Electoral College.

8) The phrase included by the Framers in the Preamble to the Constitution, "in order to form a more perfect union," reflects the concerns, which were corrected by the new Constitution, the Framers had with the

a. Declaration of Independence.
b. New Jersey Plan.
c. Federalist Papers.
d. Articles of Confederation.

9) The powers vested in Congress by the Framers to govern the nation are enumerated in
a. Article I, section 8.
b. the Preamble to the Constitution.
c. Article II.
d. the Supremacy Clause of Article VI.

10) Over the course of the nation's history under the Constitution, tremendous congressional activity expanded the powers of the federal government to accommodate changing needs and times. This expansion was undertaken by the authority vested in Congress by
a. the Bill of Rights.
b. the necessary and proper clause.
c. the judiciary clause.
d. the full faith and credit clause.

11) Article III establishes
a. the power of judicial review.
b. the Supreme Court.
c. the commander in chief powers.
d. judiciary systems of the state courts.

12) Article VI includes the supremacy clause and also requires
a. that the federal government create no ex post facto laws.
b. all states to honor the laws and official acts of the other states.
c. that states may not coin money.
d. that no religious test for public office be required for holding any public office.

13) The concept that the Framers of the Constitution were motivated principally to create a new government to protect their personal economic well-being and the well-being of men of property was first proposed in a book published in 1913 by historian
a. Edmund Randolph.
b. Charles Beard.
c. Jackson Turner Main.
d. Gordon S. Wood.

14) In general, the Anti-Federalists
a. feared the power of a strong central government.
b. argued that a president would be become far too powerful.

     c.   feared the powerful new national government would usurp the individual rights and liberties of the citizens of the states.

     d.   All of the above.

15) An example of constitutional modification through social change without amendment occurred during the Great Depression with the adoption by Congress and approval by the Supreme Court of

     a.   the New Deal programs.

     b.   the doctrine of judicial review.

     c.   the Supremacy Clause.

     d.   the declaration of war against Japan.

TRUE/FALSE

1) Thomas Paine's *Common Sense* was instrumental in arousing colonists' support for the new Constitution.

2) The Articles of Confederation were written and ratified in 1776.

3) The phrase "we the people" is found prominently in the Declaration of Independence.

4) The political philosopher Montesquieu, who advocated a separation of powers and a system of checks and balances, heavily influenced the Framers of the Constitution.

5) Article I, section 8, enumerates the powers of the president to direct and manage the government of the United States.

6) The Constitution establishes federal courts to replace the states' court systems in Article III.

7) *The Federalist Papers* were designed to explain the new Constitution and encourage people to favor ratification.

8) The Twenty-Seventh Amendment gives young people, aged eighteen to twenty-one, the right to vote.

9) The Bill of Rights was added to the Constitution in part as a way to garner support from the Anti-Federalists for the ratification of the Constitution.

10) The Constitution can only be changed through a formal amendment process.

COMPARE AND CONTRAST

Stamp Act Congress and Committees of Correspondence

the First Continental Congress and the Second Continental Congress

federation and confederation

Articles of Confederation and the U.S. Constitution

Virginia Plan, New Jersey Plan, and the Great Compromise

the three main compromises at the Constitutional Convention: the nature of the legislature, the executive branch, and representation

separation of powers and federalism

separation of powers and checks and balances

Federalists and Anti-Federalists

methods of amending the Constitution

formal and informal techniques for amending the Constitution

ESSAY AND SHORT ANSWER QUESTIONS

1)   Discuss events that led up to the Declaration of Independence.

2)   What impact did the publication of *Common Sense* have on the revolutionary process?

3)   What type of government did the Articles of Confederation set up, and what powers did each institution of government have?

4)   How was slavery treated in the Constitution? Why was it treated in this way?

5)   Compare the Articles of Confederation and the Constitution.

6)   What powers did the U.S. Constitution allocate to the executive branch and why?

7)   Discuss the route that the American colonies took toward independence.

8)   Explain the Articles of Confederation, its successes, and the problems that led to its abandonment and the Constitutional Convention.

9)   Explain the "Miracle at Philadelphia" and the compromises that had to be made in order to adopt the Constitution.

10)   Discuss the controversies over the ratification of the Constitution.

11)   Fully explain the basic principles of the Constitution.

ANSWERS TO STUDY EXERCISES

multiple choice answers

1.	d	p. 30
2.	b	p. 33
3.	c	p. 34
4.	d	p. 35, 36
5.	b	p. 37
6.	d	p. 37
7.	d	p. 39
8.	d	p. 40
9.	a	p. 44
10.	b	p. 44
11.	b	p. 44
12.	d	p. 45
13.	b	p. 47
14.	d	p. 49, 50
15.	a	p. 60

true/false answers

1.	T	p. 33
2.	F	p. 35
3.	F	p. 40
4.	T	p. 40
5.	F	p. 43
6.	F	p. 44
7.	T	p. 50
8.	F	p. 52
9.	T	p. 53
10.	F	p. 56

CHAPTER 3
FEDERALISM

Chapter Goals and Learning Objectives

Early Americans inherently distrusted a strong, central government and its powers, understandably, given the problems the colonies had with the King of England. When framing their own government, they reasoned it necessary to divide power as much as possible to prevent tyranny. They accomplished this horizontally with separation of powers and checks and balances, the three branches of government divided and sharing powers under this system. They accomplished this vertically through federalism, a system in which the national government and the states share powers. Because of these two basic divisions of power, according to James Madison in the *Federalist No. 51*, "a double security arises to the rights of the people." The Founders concluded that the national government needed more power than it was allotted under the Articles of Confederation, but the Framers never intended to gut the powers of the states. Instead, they intended to divide powers so that no one branch or level of government got too powerful. The rest of U.S. history and politics has included battles over the way in which the Constitution divvies up these powers, what the vaguely worded passages mean, and the constantly shifting relationship between the national and state governments. From the ratification of the Tenth Amendment to *McCulloch* v. *Maryland*, the Civil War to the New Deal, the Reagan Revolution to the Contract with America, all the way to the expansion of the federal government to deal with terrorism, the tug of war between the federal government and the states continues unabated.

This chapter is designed to introduce you to our system of federalism. The main topic headings of the chapter are:

- The Roots of the Federal System: Governmental Powers Under the Constitution
- Federalism and the Marshall Court
- Dual Federalism: The Taney Court, Slavery, and the Civil War
- Cooperative Federalism: The New Deal and the Growth of National Government
- New Federalism: Returning Power to the States

In each section, there are certain facts and ideas that you should strive to understand. Many are in boldface type and appear in both the narrative and in the glossary at the end of the book. Other ideas, dates, facts, events, people, etc. are more difficult to pull out of the narrative. (Keep in mind that studying for objective-style tests [multiple choice, T/F] is different than studying for essay tests. See the Study Guide section on test taking for hints on study skills.)

In general, after you finish reading and studying this chapter, you should understand the following:

- The roots of the federal system and governmental powers under the Constitution
- Defining federalism under the Marshall Court
- The development of dual federalism before and after the Civil War
- Cooperative federalism and the growth of the national Government
- The return of power to the states under new federalism

Chapter Outline and Key Points

In this section, you are provided with a basic outline of the chapter and key words/points you should know. Use this outline to develop a complete outline of the material. Write the definitions or further explanations for the terms. Use the space provided in this workbook or rewrite that material in your notebook. This will help you study and remember the material in preparation for your tests, assignments, and papers.

Number of Governments in the United States (Figure 3.1)—

The Roots of the Federal System: Governmental Power Under the Constitution

federal system—

unitary system—

Federal, Confederation, and Unitary Systems of Government (Figure 3.2)—

National Powers Under the Constitution

enumerated powers—

necessary and proper clause—

implied powers—

Distribution of Governmental Power in the federal System (Figure 3.3)—

Sixteenth Amendment—

supremacy clause—

State Powers Under the Constitution

privileges and immunities clause—

Tenth Amendment—

reserve (or police) powers—

Concurrent and Denied Powers Under the Constitution

concurrent powers—

powers denied the states under Article I—

powers denied Congress under Article I—

bill of attainder—

ex post facto law—

Relations Among the States

full faith and credit clause—

disputes between states settled by Supreme Court—

Violence Against Women Act—

extradition—

interstate compacts—

Relations Within the States

the Constitution and local governments—

Federalism and the Marshall Court

John Marshall—

McCulloch v. *Maryland* (1819)

McCulloch v. *Maryland*—

necessary and proper clause today—

Gibbons v. *Ogden* (1824)

Gibbons v. *Ogden*—

commerce clause—

Dual Federalism: The Taney Court, Slavery, and the Civil War

Roger B. Taney—

dual federalism—

Dred Scott and the Advent of Civil War

Dred Scott v. *Sandford* (1857)—

Missouri Compromise—

The Civil War, Its Aftermath, and the Continuation of Dual Federalism

Civil War Amendments—

Plessy v. *Ferguson* (1896)—

Supreme Court adherence to dual federalism—

Interstate Commerce Act and Sherman Anti-Trust Act—

Setting the State for a Stronger National Government

Sixteenth Amendment—

Seventeenth Amendment—

Cooperative Federalism: The New Deal and the Growth of National Government

the end of dual federalism—

economic events in the 1920s as catalyst for end of dual federalism—

The New Deal

Franklin D. Roosevelt—

New Deal—

"alphabetocracy"—

the Supreme Court's *laissez-faire* attitude toward the economy—

FDR's Court-packing plan—

Court reverses itself on anti-New Deal decisions—

local governments' participation in the New Deal—

The Changing Nature of Federalism: From Layer Cake to Marble Cake

layer cake metaphor—

marble cake metaphor—

cooperative federalism—

Federal Grants and National Efforts to Influence the States

Morrill Land Grant Act of 1862—

federal grant-in-aid programs—

categorical grants—

Lyndon B. Johnson—

Great Society—

"War on Poverty"—

New Federalism: Returning Power to the States

new federalism—

The Reagan Revolution

Republican "Reagan Revolution"—

massive cuts in federal domestic programs—

block grants—

The Devolution Revolution

Contract with America—

Newt Gingrich—

"devolution revolution"—

104th Congress—

unfunded mandates—

welfare changes in 1996—

Federalism Under the Bush Administration

George W. Bush—

state budget shortfalls—

federal budget deficit—

Department of Homeland Security—

"No Child Left Behind"—

preemption—

The Supreme Court: A Return to States' Rights?

Republican appointees to the federal courts—

"a new kind of judicial federalism"—

Webster (1989) and *Casey* (1992) cases illustrative of trend—

U.S. v. *Lopez* (1995)—

sovereign immunity—

1996 Supreme Court decision of Indian tribes and gaming—

other Supreme Court cases constraining federal power—

Rehnquist decision on FMLA and Nevada—

Research Ideas and Possible Paper Topics

1)   Read the *Federalist Papers* on the topic of federalism. Note down the important features of federalism and its intent. Next do some research on federalism today.

How well does what you see today conform to the "intent of the Founding Fathers"? In a paper discuss your conclusions and why you think federalism today is similar to or different than what was envisioned in 1787.

2) Using the library or the Internet, find information on another federal system and compare its division of powers to the United States'. What can such a comparison tell us about our system of government?

3) What do you think are the most important federal issues today and why? Some possibilities include "full faith and credit—"particularly regarding same sex marriages and tinted windows in cars—the use of the "commerce clause", reproductive rights, term limits, child support issues, and many others.

4) Consider this idea and be prepared to argue in favor or against:
"Federalism, the separation of powers, and checks and balances are all institutional arrangements designed to make government move in a slow and cumbersome manner—in other words, the gridlock we often complain about is intentional—so that the government cannot infringe on our rights and liberties. If we had an efficient government, our liberties would be greatly reduced."

5) Research and analyze the growth of the presidency and, in turn, the national government under the administration of Franklin D. Roosevelt and discuss how his presidency launch the expansion of federal power over state governments, which culminated with the presidency of Lyndon B. Johnson.

Web Sites

National Council of State Legislators site offers analyses and information on intergovernmental relations.
www.ncsl.org/statefed/afipolcy.htm

NGA On-Line. The **National Governors' Council is** a nonpartisan organization that looks at solving state-focused problems and provides information on state innovations and practices. The Web site has stories and articles of interest on the states and provides links to similar issues and organizations.
www.nga.org/nga/1,1169,00.html

Center for the Study of Federalism at Temple University. The Center publishes *Publius: The Journal of Federalism* and *The Federalism Report* and the Web site offers a variety of links as well.
www.temple.edu/federalism/

Publius: The Journal of Federalism. *Publius,* published by Lafayette College, offers academic articles on federal issues in the U.S. and abroad. They do periodic special issues on the state of federalism in the U.S.

http://ww2.lafayette.edu/~publius/

The General Services Administration gives you the ability to search for information on hundreds of federal grants.
www.gsa.gov

The Brookings Institution, a moderate-to-liberal think-tank in Washington, has a policy brief on federalism titled: "Waive of the Future? Federalism and the Next Phase of Welfare Reform"
http://www.brookings.edu/es/research/projects/wrb/publications/pb/pb29.htm

American Enterprise Institute, a conservative think-tank, conducts the Federalism Project, which "explores opportunities to restore real federalism—that is, a federalism that limits the national government's power and competes for their citizens' assets, talents, and business."
http://www.federalismproject.org/

The Urban Institute, a "nonprofit policy research organization established in Washington D.C. in 1968" has prepared a number of articles and reports relating to federalism under the heading "Assessing the New Federalism."
www.urban.org/content/Research/NewFederalism/AboutANF/AboutANF.htm

The Constitution Society provides access to the text of the Federalist papers as well as links to other sites relating to states' rights.
www.constitution.org/cs_feder.htm

The Nelson A. Rockefeller Institute of Government at the State University of New York conducts research on the role of state and local government in American federalism and on the management and finances of states and localities.
www.rockinst.org

This site from **Infidels.org** contains links to articles and organizations with information on federalism.
www.infidels.org/~nap/index.federalism.html

A **Find Law** online article entitled "How Federalism Doctrine Can Acquire Bipartisan Appeal: The Constitutional Values That Transcend Political Change" discusses the New Federalism approach of the Rehnquist Court.
http://writ.news.findlaw.com/commentary/20041210_brownstein.html

MULTIPLE CHOICE

1) While most of the delegates to the Constitutional Convention in Philadelphia favored a strong national government, they realized that some compromises regarding the distribution of powers would be necessary, and therefore created
    a.   a confederate form of government very similar to one that had existed under the original constitution, the Articles of Confederation.
    b.   a highly centralized form of government, similar to Great Britain's.
    c.   a direct democracy.
    d.   the world's first federal system, in which the states were bound together under one national government.

2) A power that is not stated explicitly in the Constitution but is considered to reasonably flow from a power stated in Article I, section 8, is called a(n)
    a.   derivative power.
    b.   implied power.
    c.   enumerated power.
    d.   concurrent power.

3) When is the supremacy clause applicable?
    a.   when a state and national law concur
    b.   when a state law exists where no national law exists
    c.   when state and national law conflict
    d.   when a law passed by Congress conflicts with god-given rights

4) The Sixteenth Amendment to the Constitution, adopted in 1913, gave what power to the national government that had not existed under the original Constitution?
    a.   the power to levy taxes
    b.   the power to borrow money
    c.   the power to tax personal income nationally
    d.   the power to regulate intrastate commerce

5) The guarantee of states' rights was provided in the Constitution by
    a.   Article I, section 8.
    b.   the supremacy clause.
    c.   the necessary and proper clause.
    d.   the Tenth Amendment.

6) Article I denies certain powers to the national and state governments, including
    a.   passing bills of attainder.
    b.   entering into contracts.
    c.   involvement in elections.

d.   the power to tax.

7)   Article IV requires that states recognize judicial proceedings, records, and laws of
      other states. This is known as the _____ clause.
      a.   commerce
      b.   full faith and credit
      c.   contract
      d.   necessary and proper

8)   The first major decision of the Marshall Court (in 1819) to define the federal
      relationship between the national government and the states (by upholding the
      necessary and proper clause and the supremacy clause) was
      a.   *Marbury* v. *Madison.*
      b.   *Gibbons* v. *Ogden.*
      c.   *McCulloch* v. *Maryland.*
      d.   *Dred Scott* v. *Sandford.*

9)   The Supreme Court ruled in 1824 that Congress had wide authority under the
      commerce clause to regulate interstate commerce, including commercial activity,
      in
      a.   *Marshall* v. *New York.*
      b.   *Gibbons* v. *Ogden.*
      c.   *McCulloch* v. *Maryland.*
      d.   *Fulton* v. *New Jersey.*

10)   In 1937, the Supreme Court reversed its series of decisions against New Deal
      programs, afterward approving broad extensions of the use by Congress of the
      commerce clause to regulate and bolster the economy. The Supreme Court
      reversed its anti-New Deal trend as a result of
      a.   the worsening of Great Depression conditions.
      b.   the increased participation of city government in federal affairs.
      c.   the imminent threat of war with Nazi Germany and Imperial Japan.
      d.   the threat of the Roosevelt court-packing plan.

11)   The type of federalism metaphorically referred to as "marble cake" federalism is
      known as _____ federalism.
      a.   cooperative
      b.   dual
      c.   competitive
      d.   mixed

12)   A broad grant of monies given to states with few qualifications or restrictions by
      the federal government for specified activities is called a _____ grant.
      a.   creative
      b.   categorical
      c.   block

d. federal

13) The practice of the federal government overriding state actions in some areas is called
   a. supremacy.
   b. preemption.
   c. confiscation.
   d. mediation.

14) The 1995 Supreme Court case, *U.S.* v. *Lopez* is significant because it was the first decision by the Court in many decades in which it
   a. restrained Congress's use of the commerce power, thus shifting power from the national government to the states.
   b. expanded Congress's use of the commerce clause in enhancing federal power.
   c. questioned the use of the power of judicial review by the Court.
   d. declared that federal preemption was unconstitutional.

15) Despite the trend of the Rehnquist Court to limit and reverse the expansion of the federal government's power, the Rehnquist Court in 2002 supported the federal government's contention that its law was an appropriate exercise of Congress's power over the states with regard to the federal
   a. Religious Freedom Restoration Act.
   b. Family and Medical Leave Act.
   c. gun control law regulating weapons in public schools.
   d. law requiring states to negotiate with Indian tribes about gaming.

TRUE/FALSE

1) More than 87,000 state and local governments are bound by the provisions of the Constitution.

2) The Framers chose federalism to imitate the British highly centralized governmental system.

3) Article I of the Constitution gives Congress the explicit power to tax, including the power to levy a national personal income tax.

4) The Supremacy Clause states that all powers not specifically granted in the Constitution are reserved to the states.

5) Police powers are among those powers reserved to the states.

6) Legal controversies between the states can be decided only by the U.S. Supreme Court.

7) The Supreme Court decision in the *Dred Scott* case contributed to the advent of the Civil War.

8) The Civil War forever changed the nature of federalism.

9) The adoption of the Civil War Amendments guaranteed the absolute sovereignty of state power.

10) The first federal grant program, the Morrill Land Grant Act, was created in response to the Great Depression.

COMPARE AND CONTRAST

powers of the national government, concurrent powers, and powers of the state governments

enumerated, implied, and denied powers

supremacy clause and reserve (police) powers

Dual Federalism and Cooperative Federalism

Layer Cake and Marble Cake Federalism

categorical and block grants

ESSAY AND SHORT ANSWER QUESTIONS

1) Why did the Framers choose federalism? (Hint: Remember to define federalism.)

2) Discuss the nature and ramifications of the supremacy clause.

3) Explain the doctrine of implied powers.

4) What is the role of the states in our federal system? How is it dealt with in the Constitution?

5) Describe the nature of relations among the states.

6) Explain the distribution of power in the federal system.

7) Discuss how *McCulloch v. Maryland* and *Gibbons v. Ogden* contributed to the development of federalism. Be sure to include the facts and ruling in each case.

8) Discuss the various stages of federalism this country has gone through from dual federalism to today. What does the evolution of federalism tell us about our system?

9) Explain the uses of preemption and unfunded mandates. How have these methods been used to alter the nature of federalism, and what is their current status?

10) Explain the changing nature of federalism.

ANSWERS TO STUDY EXERCISES

multiple choice answers

1.	d	p. 101, 102
2.	b	p. 104
3.	c	p. 106
4.	c	p. 106
5.	d	p. 106
6.	a	p. 108
7.	b	p. 108
8.	c	p. 110
9.	b	p. 112
10.	d	p. 116
11.	a	p. 117
12.	c	p. 119
13.	b	p. 124
14.	a	p. 126
15.	b	p. 127

true/false answers

1.	T	p. 102
2.	F	p. 103
3.	F	p. 104
4.	F	p. 106
5.	T	p. 106
6.	T	p. 108
7.	T	p. 113
8.	T	p. 113
9.	F	p. 113
10.	F	p. 117

CHAPTER 4
CIVIL LIBERTIES

Chapter Goals and Learning Objectives

Civil liberties are the individual rights and freedoms listed in the Bill of Rights that the federal government cannot abridge, liberties which are protected from the "tyranny of the majority" and the excesses of the government. The Bill of Rights places limits on the power of government to restrain or dictate how people may express themselves and act. The civil liberties we possess, however, are not absolute nor are these liberties simple to explain and understand. They are interpreted and reinterpreted by the Supreme Court and common practice over time. The Bill of Rights originally protected the civil liberties of citizens only from their national government. Subsequently, following the adoption of the Fourteenth Amendment and through the use of the doctrine of selective incorporation, the Supreme Court passed most of the Bill of Rights protections onto the states, thus protecting citizens from their state governments as well as the federal government. The Court tries to balance rights between competing interests. For example, the Court has generally ruled that your right to free speech ends when you incite a riot that would cause immediate physical harm to others. Here the Court balances an individual's right with the rights of the public at large. Each liberty interest faces a similar balancing act in its interpretation. In this chapter, we explore what the government may and may not do and which interests are being balanced at a given time.

This chapter is designed to inform you about the individual rights and freedoms granted to you by the Bill of Rights. The main topic headings of the chapter are:

- The First Constitutional Amendments: The Bill of Rights
- First Amendment Guarantees: Freedom of Religion
- First Amendment Guarantees: Freedom of Speech, Press, and Assembly
- The Second Amendment: The Right to Keep and Bear Arms
- The Rights of Criminal Defendants
- The Right to Privacy

In each section, there are certain facts and ideas that you should strive to understand. Many are in boldface type and appear in both the narrative and in the glossary at the end of the book. Other ideas, dates, facts, events, people, etc. are more difficult to pull out of the narrative. (Keep in mind that studying for objective-style tests [multiple choice, T/F] is different than studying for essay tests. See the Study Guide section on test taking for hints on study skills.)

In general, after you finish reading and studying this chapter, you should understand the following:

- The Bill of Rights and the reasons for its addition to the Constitution
- The application of some rights in the Bill of Rights to the states via the incorporation doctrine
- The meaning of the First Amendment's guarantee of freedom of religion in the establishment clause and free exercise clause
- The meaning of the First Amendment's guarantees of freedom of speech, press, and assembly
- The interpretation and controversy over the Second Amendment; the right to keep and bear arms
- Rights of the accused or criminal defendant's rights in the Fourth, Fifth, Sixth, and Eighth Amendments and how the U.S. Supreme Court has expanded and contracted those rights
- The meaning of the right to privacy and how it has been interpreted by the Court

---

Chapter Outline and Key Points

In this section, you are provided with a basic outline of the chapter and key words/points you should know. Use this outline to develop a complete outline of the material. Write the definitions or further explanations for the terms. Use the space provided in this workbook or rewrite that material in your notebook. This will help you study and remember the material in preparation for your tests, assignments, and papers.

civil liberties—

civil rights—

The First Constitutional Amendments: The Bill of Rights

George Mason's proposal during the Constitutional Convention—

Federalists arguments against a bill of rights—

Anti-Federalists insistence on inclusion of bill of rights—

Bill of Rights—

Ninth Amendment—

Tenth Amendment—

**The Incorporation Doctrine: The Bill of Rights Made Applicable
to the States**

Barron v. *Baltimore* (1833)—

Fourteenth Amendment—

due process clause—

substantive due process—

Gitlow v. *NewYork* (1925)—

Near v. *Minnesota* (1931)—

selective incorporation—

Selective Incorporation and Fundamental Freedoms

Palko v. *Connecticut* (1937)—

fundamental rights—

The Selective Incorporation of the Bill of Rights (Table 4.1)—

<u>First Amendment Guarantees: Freedom of Religion</u>

poll data that America is one of the most religions nations in the world—

Article VI "no religious test"—

First Amendment—

establishment clause—

wall of separation—

free exercise clause—

The Establishment Clause

Engel v. *Vitale* (1962)—

prayer at high school football games and moment of silence—

"under God" in Pledge of Allegiance—

Lemon v. *Kurtzman* (1971)—

three-part *Lemon* test for establishment issues:

    1)—

    2)—

    3)—

how the Court subsequently sidesteps the *Lemon* test—

1995 case involving Christian group at a university denied funding for student magazine—

Zelman v. *Simmons-Harris* (2002)—

The Free Exercise Clause

how free exercise clause is not absolute—

1990 Oregon peyote case—

Congress passes Religious Freedom Restoration Act and Supreme Court overturns it—

First Amendment Guarantees: Freedom of Speech, Press, and Assembly

demand by some to limit free speech in society—

Freedom of Speech and Press

free exchange of ideas—

Supreme Court's protection of thoughts, actions, and words—

The Alien and Sedition Acts—

    prior restraint—

Slavery, the Civil War, and Rights Curtailment—

    Lincoln's suppression of First Amendment during Civil War—

    Ex parte McCardle (1869)—

World War I and Anti-Governmental Speech—

Espionage Act of 1917—

Schenck v. *U.S.* (1919)—

clear and present danger test—

Brandenburg v. *Ohio* (1969)—

direct incitement test—

Protected Speech and Publications

Prior Restraint—

New York Times v. *United States* (1971)—

Symbolic Speech—

symbolic speech—

Stomberg v. *California* (1931)—

Tinker v. *Des Moines Independent Community School District* (1969)—

1989 flag burning case—

Federal Flag Protection Act of 1989 and Supreme Court overturning a conviction based upon it—

Hate Speech, Unpopular Speech, and Speech Zones—

R.A.V. v. *City of St. Paul* (1992)—

free speech zones—

Unprotected Speech and Publications

Libel and Slander—

libel—

slander—

New York Times v. *Sullivan* (1971)—

actual malice—

Fighting Words—

Chaplinsky v. *New Hampshire* (1942)—

1968 Cohen case ("Fuck the Draft. Stop the War")—

Obscenity—

Roth v. *U.S.* (1957)—

Miller v. *California* (1973)—

Miller test—

Congress and Obscenity—

NEA and Congress—

Communications Decency Act of 1996—

Reno v. *ACLU* (1997)—

Child Online Protection Act of 1998—

Ashcroft v. *Free Speech Coalition* (2002)—

Freedoms of Assembly and Petition—

DeJonge v. *Oregon* (1937)—

The Second Amendment: The Right to Keep and Bear Arms

local colonial militias—

Second Amendment—

U.S. v. *Miller* (1939)—

Quilici v. *Village of Morton* (1983)—

Brady Bill—

National Rifle Association—

The Rights of Criminal Defendants

due process rights (also known as procedural guarantees, rights of defendants)—

The Fourth Amendment and Searches and Seizures

Fourth Amendment—

Supreme Court has interpreted Fourth Amendment to allow the police to search:

       1)—

       2)—

       3)—

knock and announce—

reasonable suspicion—

warrantless searches—

stop and frisk—

probable cause—

search warrant—

"open fields doctrine"—

automobile searches—

Detainees (p. 152)—

Drug Testing—

      drug testing in high schools—

      drug testing and pregnant women—

The Fifth Amendment and Self-Incrimination

Fifth Amendment—

self-incrimination—

use of voluntary confessions—

Miranda v. *Arizona* (1966)—

Miranda rights—

The Fourth and Fifth Amendments and the Exclusionary Rule

Weeks v. *U.S.* (1914)—

exclusionary rule—

"fruits of a poisonous tree"—

Mapp v. *Ohio* (1961)—

good faith exception—

inevitable discovery—

The Sixth Amendment and Right to Counsel

Sixth Amendment—

Gideon v. *Wainwright* (1963)—

actual imprisonment standard—

The Sixth Amendment and Jury Trials

Sixth Amendment—

impartial jury—

Batson v. *Kentucky* (1986)—

Maryland v. *Craig* (1990)—

47

The Eighth Amendment and Cruel and Unusual Punishment

Eighth Amendment—

Furman v. *Georgia* (1972)—

Gregg v. *Georgia* (1976)—

Illinois Governor George Ryan moratorium on executions—

The Right to Privacy

right to privacy—

Birth Control

Griswold v. *Connecticut* (1965)—

"penumbras" of the Constitution—

Abortion

Roe v. *Wade* (1973)—

Webster v. *Reproductive Health Services* (1989)—

Planned Parenthood of Southeastern Pennsylvania v. *Casey* (1992)—

"undue burden"—

Stenberg v. *Carhart* (2000)—

Partial Birth Abortion Ban Act of 2003—

Homosexuality

Lawrence v. *Texas* (2003)—

The Right to Die

1997 Supreme Court case on physician-assisted suicide (*Vacco* v. *Quill*)—

U.S. Attorney General Ashcroft and Oregon assisted suicide law—

Research Ideas and Possible Paper Topics

1) Find out if your campus has a "speech code." (If it doesn't, find a nearby college or university with one.) Would this code stand up to a constitutional test? Why or why not? According to your understanding of the First Amendment, are speech codes constitutional? Do some research at the campus newspaper and see if there was any controversy surrounding the adoption of the speech code and discuss it in class.

2) Explore the current docket of the Supreme Court. What civil liberties issues are going to be or are being heard this term? How do you think they will be decided and why? Follow the process until the rulings are made and see if you are right.

3) Under Chief Justice Rehnquist, the Court has reduced many of the due process rights granted under the Warren and Burger Courts. Find examples of how these rights have changed and why. What has the role of public and political opinion been in these changes?

4) Contact your local branch of the American Civil Liberties Union. Visit or ask for written information about their activities and issues. Find out what they do and why. Also check their Web site (see below) for information.

5) The 2003 Supreme Court decision in *Lawrence* v. *Texas* has far-reaching implications for gay rights in the United States. The *Lawrence* decision precipitated activity, for example, in the states and in national politics regarding same-sex marriages. What effects did the *Lawrence* decision have on that and other issues relating to gay rights and American politics?

Web Sites

The **Legal Information Institute** of Cornell University has an excellent site that offers extensive information about civil liberties. There is a section focused on the First Amendment with definitions, historical background, Supreme Court decisions, and links to numerous First Amendment-related sites. There are also sites at LII for prisoners' rights, employment rights, and constitutional rights generally.
www.law.cornell.edu/topics/first_amendment.html

American Civil Liberties Union (ACLU) offers information on the entire Bill of Rights including racial profiling, women's rights, privacy issues, prisons, drugs, etc. Includes links to other sites dealing with the same issues.
www.aclu.org

The U.S. Information Agency of the Department of State offers an annotated version of the full text of the Bill of Rights and other constitutional documents.

http://usinfo.state.gov/products/pubs/constitution/amendment.htm

The **Cato Institute,** a Libertarian think-tank, hosts a Constitution Studies page on its Web site, examining Amendments 1, 2, 4, 5, 9 and 10 as well as other constitutional issues.

www.cato.org/ccs/issues.html

First Amendment Cyber-Tribune (FACT) is a Web site hosted by the Casper Star-Tribune and is an extensive resource on the many liberty guarantees of the First Amendment. The site is continually updated and expanded.

http://w3.trib.com/FACT/

PBS offers a Web page that presents the background and issues relating to *Texas* v. *Johnson* and *U.S.* v. *Eichman*, the flag-burning cases, freedom of expression cases.

www.pbs.org/jefferson/enlight/flag.htm

Freedom Forum is an organization that studies and reports on First Amendment issues, particularly matters relating to freedom of the press.

http://www.firstamendmentcenter.org

Americans United for Separation of Church and State monitors church-state separation issues and promotes protection of the First Amendment establishment clause in Congress and state legislatures.

www.au.org

Professor Eugene Volkh of the **UCLA Law School** maintains a list of links to sources on the Second Amendment. You can also click on a link to his homepage to find a list of scholarly articles he has written on the Second Amendment and other Bill of Rights issues.

http://www1.law.ucla.edu/~volokh/2amteach/sources.htm

The James Madison Research Library and Information Center Web site is hosted by **The National Rifle Association** to detail their understanding of the Second Amendment.

www.madisonbrigade.com

The Brady Campaign to Prevent Gun Violence, created by Nancy Brady after the debilitating gunshot wound to her husband, James Brady, during the Reagan assassination attempt, hosts a Web site detailing their national fight against the NRA to enact gun control measures in Congress and the state legislatures. The Second Amendment page on the site contends that the NRA is wrong in its interpretation of history and Supreme Court decisions that individual private gun ownership is broadly protected by the Second Amendment.

www.handguncontrol.org/facts/issuebriefs/second.asp

Fighting Terrorism/Protecting Liberty is a site by the **National Association of Criminal Defense Lawyers.** This site monitors the many bills in Congress and proposals by the Department of Justice to increase the powers of law enforcement in the face of terrorism. The NACDL and other organizations concerned with civil liberties track these measures to ensure the least possible intrusion on liberties consistent with protection from terrorist attacks.
> www.criminaljustice.org/public.nsf/freeform/terrorism1?OpenDocument

Also from the **National Association of Criminal Defense Lawyers** is a Web page devoted to the fortieth anniversary in 2003 of the Supreme Court decision in *Gideon* v. *Wainwright.*
> http://www.nacdl.org/gideon

NoloPress provides a Web page that offers a tour of the ways in which the Bill of Rights attempts to ensure fair treatment for those accused of crimes by the government.
> http://www.nolo.com/lawcenter/ency/article.cfm/objectID/6410CC94-3E8F-
> 4A37-A5F85E3348E6431F/catID/D4C65461-8D33-482C-
> 92FCEA7F2ADED29A

The Center for Reproductive Rights Web site has an extensive guide to national and international legal issues dealing with abortion.
> http://www.crlp.org

The American Life League Web site has a list of Supreme Court cases and links to information regarding the abortion issue from a pro-life position.
> www.all.org/issues/abscotus.htm

The University of Missouri-Kansas City School of Law hosts a Web page with background of Supreme Court cases dealing with gay rights in the United States.
> http://www.law.umkc.edu/faculty/projects/ftrials/conlaw/gayrights.htm

A Web site published by the **University of Washington Libraries** titled *Taking Back America* provides numerous links about the USA Patriot Act and treats to the liberty interests of American citizens raised by the Act.
> http://www.lib.washington.edu/Suzref/patriot-act/

Findlaw is a searchable database of S.C. decisions plus legal subjects, state courts, law schools, bar associations, and international law.
> www.findlaw.com

MULTIPLE CHOICE

1) The Bill of Rights, as added to the Constitution originally,
   a. was a compromise between the Federalists and the Anti-Federalists.
   b. listed a number of individual and states' rights to be protected.
   c. was designed to serve as protection against infringement of rights by the new national government.
   d. All of the above.

2) The Constitution was ratified in 1789; Amendments 1 through 10 were ratified
   a. over the course of 20 years, following the adoption of the Constitution.
   b. in 1789 (Amendments 1-5) and 1792 (Amendment 6-10).
   c. in 1791.
   d. in 1789.

3) The Supreme Court ruled that the Bill of Rights limited only the federal government and not the states in
   a. *Barron* v. *Baltimore.*
   b. *McCulloch* v. *Maryland.*
   c. *Cantwell* v. *Connecticut.*
   d. *Reynolds* v. *U.S.*

4) The due process clause is located in the _____ Amendment(s).
   a. Fifth
   b. Sixth
   c. Fourteenth
   d. Fifth and Fourteenth

5) The rationale for the process of selective incorporation protecting against the abridgment only of fundamental freedoms was set out in the 1937 Supreme Court case of
   a. *Cantwell* v. *Connecticut.*
   b. *Reynolds* v. *Sims.*
   c. *Near* v. *Minnesota.*
   d. *Palko* v. *Connecticut.*

6) The clause in the Bill of Rights that prohibits the national government from establishing an official religion is called the
   a. establishment clause.
   b. free exercise clause.
   c. religious freedom clause.
   d. freedom to choose clause.

7) The Supreme Court has ruled that in establishment clause questions, a law is constitutional if it had a secular purpose, neither advanced nor inhibited religion, and did not foster excessive government entanglement with religion. The ruling comes from the case
   a. *Mapp* v. *Ohio.*
   b. *Lemon* v. *Kurtzman.*
   c. *Stenburg* v. *Carhart.*
   d. *Chaplinsky* v. *New Hampshire.*

8) The Supreme Court first acknowledged symbolic speech in the case
   a. *Chaplinsky* v. *New Hampshire.*
   b. *Roth* v. *U.S.*
   c. *Stromberg* v. *California.*
   d. *Miller* v. *California.*

9) Which of the following is protected by the First Amendment guarantee of freedom of speech?
   a. fighting words
   b. slander and libel
   c. obscenity
   d. burning of the American flag

10) The amendment that requires the police to get a search warrant to conduct searches of your home in most cases is the _____ Amendment.
    a. Fourth
    b. Fifth
    c. Sixth
    d. Eighth

11) In 1966, the Court ruled that suspects must be apprised of their rights once arrested in the case of
    a. *Gideon* v. *Wainwright.*
    b. *Michigan* v. *Tyler.*
    c. *Mapp* v. *Ohio.*
    d. *Miranda* v. *Arizona.*

12) In *Weeks* v. *U.S.* (1914), the Supreme Court barred the use of illegally seized evidence at trial. This is called the
    a. warrant rule.
    b. exclusionary rule.
    c. Weeks test.
    d. search and seizure doctrine.

13) Death penalty cases are usually dealt with under the _____ Amendment.
    a. Fourth
    b. Fifth

c.	Sixth
d.	Eighth

14)	The right to privacy was first cited in
a.	*Furman* v. *Georgia.*
b.	*McCleskey* v. *Zant.*
c.	*Griswold* v. *Connecticut.*
d.	*Roe* v. *Wade.*

15)	Where is the right to privacy found in the U.S. Constitution?
a.	in the Fourth Amendment
b.	in the Sixth Amendment
c.	in the "Right to Privacy Amendment"
d.	in the "penumbras" of the Constitution

TRUE/FALSE

1)	The Federalists put forward the idea of a Bill of Rights in order to protect the liberty of individual citizens from the state governments.

2)	The Court first ruled that state-sponsored prayer in public school was unconstitutional in *Engel* v. *Vitale.*

3)	In *New York Times* v. *United States*, the Supreme Court ruled that the U.S. government could, under any circumstance, prevent the publication of papers or information regarding national security.

4)	Burning the American flag is considered constitutionally protected symbolic speech.

5)	*New York Times* v. *Sullivan* made it much easier to prove libel against public figures.

6)	The Fourth Amendment's purpose was to deny the national government the authority to conduct general searches.

7)	Police officers do not need a warrant if they have consent to search.

8)	The Sixth Amendment guarantees citizens an attorney under all circumstances, even if it is not a criminal case.

9)	The right to privacy clause is located in the Fourteenth Amendment.

10)	The 2003 Supreme Court decision in *Lawrence* v. *Texas* held that a Texas law prohibiting abortion violated fundamental privacy rights under the Constitution.

COMPARE AND CONTRAST

civil liberties and civil rights

the Bill of Rights and the Incorporation Doctrine

free exercise and establishment clause

clear and present danger and direct incitement tests

symbolic speech, prior restraint, and hate speech

due process rights: Fourth, Fifth, Sixth and Eighth Amendments

Furman v. *Georgia, Gregg* v. *Georgia,* and *McCleskey* v. *Kemp*

Privacy Rights: birth control, abortion, homosexual rights, the right to die, medical records, etc.

ESSAY AND SHORT ANSWER QUESTIONS

1) What is the Bill of Rights, and why was it added to the Constitution?

2) Explain the establishment clause and its current application.

3) What is the incorporation doctrine, and how has it been used?

4) What is the exclusionary rule, and why is it important?

5) What has the Supreme Court ruled in "right to die" cases?

6) Explain the First Amendment. What rights and liberties are covered by this amendment, how has the Supreme Court interpreted its meanings, and what rights/liberties is the Court trying to balance in making its rulings on these issues? Be sure to cite cases.

7) Explain our rights to free speech, freedom of the press, and freedom to petition and assemble. What limits exist on these rights? Be sure to cite cases.

8) Discuss the Fourth Amendment fully. Cite cases.

9)   Discuss due process rights stemming from the Fifth, Sixth, and Eighth Amendments. How have these protections changed over time? Be sure to cite cases.

10)   What is the right to privacy? What are the constitutional bases of this right? How has this right been applied and to what might it be applied in the future?

ANSWERS TO STUDY EXERCISES

multiple choice answers

1.	d	p. 132
2.	c	p. 132
3.	a	p. 132
4.	d	p. 132
5.	d	p. 133
6.	a	p. 135
7.	b	p. 135, 136
8.	c	p. 144
9.	d	p. 144, 145
10.	d	p. 150
11.	d	p. 153
12.	b	p. 154
13.	d	p. 157
14.	c	p. 158
15.	d	p. 158

true/false answers

1.	F	p. 131, 132
2.	T	p. 135
3.	F	p. 141
4.	T	p. 144
5.	F	p. 145
6.	T	p. 150
7.	T	p. 151
8.	F	p. 156
9.	F	p. 158
10.	F	p. 161

CHAPTER 5
CIVIL RIGHTS

Chapter Goals and Learning Objectives

Civil rights concern the positive acts that governments take to protect individuals against arbitrary or discriminatory treatment, by government or individuals. The Framers were most concerned with creating a new, workable, and enduring form of government than with civil rights. The Fourteenth Amendment introduced the idea of equal protection of the laws and has generated more litigation to determine and specify its meaning than any other constitutional provision. This chapter explores how African Americans, women, and other disadvantaged political groups have drawn ideas, support and success from one another in the quest for equality under the law.

This chapter is designed to inform you about the struggle of women and minorities for civil rights and the privileges of citizenship, including equal protection of the laws and voting rights. The main topic headings of the chapter are:

- Slavery, Abolition, and Winning the Right to Vote, 1800-1890
- The Push for Equality, 1890-1954
- The Civil Rights Movement
- The Women's Rights Movement
- Other Groups Mobilize for Rights
- Continuing Controversies in Civil Rights

In each section, there are certain facts and ideas that you should strive to understand. Many are in boldface type and appear in both the narrative and in the glossary at the end of the book. Other ideas, dates, facts, events, people, etc. are more difficult to pull out of the narrative. (Keep in mind that studying for objective-style tests [multiple choice, T/F] is different than studying for essay tests. See the Study Guide section on test taking for hints on study skills.)

In general, after you finish reading and studying this chapter, you should understand the following:

- Slavery, abolition, and winning the right to vote from 1800 to 1890
- The push for equality by African Americans and women from 1885 to 1954
- The Civil Rights Act of 1964 and its facilitation and effects
- The development of a new women's rights movement
- The push for an equal rights amendment
- Efforts of other groups to expand the definition of civil rights further such as Native Americans, Hispanic Americans, Gays and Lesbians, and Disabled Americans
- Continuing controversies in civil rights, including affirmative action

In this section, you are provided with a basic outline of the chapter and key words/points you should know. Use this outline to develop a complete outline of the material. Write the definitions or further explanations for the terms. Use the space provided in this workbook or rewrite that material in your notebook. This will help you study and remember the material in preparation for your tests, assignments, and papers.

civil rights—

Fourteenth Amendment—

Slavery, Abolition, and Winning the Right to Vote, 1800-1890

Slavery and Congress

Missouri Compromise of 1820—

The First Civil Rights Movements: Abolition and Women's Rights

abolitionist movement—

NAACP—

Frederick Douglass—

Seneca Falls Convention (1848)—

The 1850s: The Calm Before the Storm

Uncle Tom's Cabin (1852)—

Dred Scott v. *Sandford* (1857)—

The Civil War and its Aftermath: Civil Rights Laws and Constitutional Amendments

Emancipation Proclamation—

Thirteenth Amendment—

Black Codes—

Civil Rights Act of 1866—

Fourteenth Amendment—

Fifteenth Amendment—

disappointment of women's rights movement over Fourteenth and Fifteenth amendments—

Civil Rights, Congress, and the Supreme Court

Civil Rights Act of 1875—

Civil Rights Cases (1883)—

The Slaughterhouse Cases (1873)—

three ways Southern states excluded African Americans from the vote after the Civil War Amendments:

   1) poll taxes—

   2) property-owning qualifications—

   3) literacy tests—

grandfather clause—

The Push for Equality, 1890-1954

Plessy v. *Ferguson* (1896)—

separate but equal—

The Founding of Key Groups

NAACP—

NAWSA—

suffrage movement—

Nineteenth Amendment—

W.E.B. DuBois—

Litigating for Equality

Test Cases—

white-only schools—

Lloyd Gaines case of 1938—

NAACP-LDF—

Thurgood Marshall—

H.W. Sweatt and the University of Texas—

amicus curiae briefs—

Brown v. *Board of Education* (1954)—

equal protection clause—

The Civil Rights Movement

School Desegregation After Brown

Brown v. *Board of Education II* (1955)—

Little Rock Central High School—

Cooper v. *Aaron* (1958)—

A New Move for African American Rights

Rosa Parks—

Montgomery Bus Boycott—

Dr. Martin Luther King, Jr.—

Formation of New Groups

Southern Christian Leadership Council (SCLC)—

Student Nonviolent Coordinating Committee (SNCC)—

sit-in protest—

freedom rides—

march on Birmingham—

The Civil Rights Act of 1964

March on Washington, August 1963—

"I Have A Dream" speech—

President Lyndon B. Johnson—

Strom Thurmond—

elements of Civil Right Act of 1964:

1)

2)

3)

4)

5)

6)

Malcolm X—

<u>The Women's Rights Movement</u>

opposition to women's rights—

1961 President's Commission on the Status of Women

Betty Friedan's *The Feminine Mystique*—

Equal Pay Act in 1963—

sex discrimination prohibition included in Civil Rights Act of 1964—

Equal Opportunity Employment Commission (EEOC)—

National Organization of Women (NOW)—

The Equal Rights Amendment

Equal Rights Amendment (ERA)—

ratification record on ERA—

Litigating for Equal Rights

The Equal Protection Clause and Constitutional Standards of Review—

rational basis test—

suspect classification—

strict scrutiny—

fundamental freedoms—

Equal Protection Clause and Standards of Review Used by the Supreme Court to Determine Whether It Has Been Violated (see Table 5.1)—

Ruth Bader Ginsburg—

Craig v. *Boren* (1976)—

practices which have been found to violate the Fourteenth Amendment—

governmental practices and laws upheld by the Court—

Statutory Remedies for Sex Discrimination—

Title VII of the Civil Rights Act—

Wage Gap, 2002 (Figure 5.1)—

key victories under Title VII—

Title IX—

Other Groups Mobilize for Rights

Hispanic Americans

largest minority group in the United States—

pattern of Hispanic population growth in United States—

MALDEF—

LULAC—

public school discrimination cases—

immigration cases—

Native Americans

"Indian tribes" under the U.S. Constitution—

Native American Rights Fund—

Department of Interior and Indian trust funds—

Gays and Lesbians

gay and lesbian activists' groups—

"Don't Ask, Don't Tell" policy—

Romer v. *Evans* (1996)—

Lawrence v. *Texas* (2003)—

gay marriage issue—

Disabled Americans

Americans with Disabilities Act (ADA) of 1990—

the cumulative effect of four 1999 Supreme Court cases on the ADA—

Continuing Controversies in Civil Rights

affirmative action—

Regents of the University of California v. *Bakke* (1978)—

Civil Rights Act of 1991 and affirmative action—

Grutter v. *Bollinger* (2002)—

gay rights activists and Cracker Barrel restaurants—

Wal-Mart discrimination against women—

Wal-Mart discrimination against immigrants—

Research Ideas and Possible Paper Topics

1) Look at the current Supreme Court docket. What civil rights cases do you see? What are their constitutional arguments, and how do they differ from the cases the book discusses in the 1950s, 60s and 70s?

2) The use of *amicus curaie* briefs has increased dramatically in the last several decades and many people now argue that public opinion plays a role in Supreme Court decisions. Analyze and discuss these two issues. How would you characterize the role of such influence in civil rights cases?

3) Examine the controversial issue of same-sex marriages and research it in-depth. What constitutional issues are used, what arguments, etc.? How did the issue effect the 2004 presidential election? How do you feel the current Court would rule on this issue and why? Explore the possibility of a constitution amendment proposed by the Republican Party to prohibit same-sex marriages.

4) Look at the current Supreme Court. Do some biographical and case research on each of the nine justices in the area of civil rights. Build a typography (classify the judges into groups of like-minded individuals) on how the current justices rule on civil rights. (Example: The simplest typography would be liberal—moderate—conservative. But be sure to define each of those categories! A more complex system would provide better analysis of the Court.) In regard to the Supreme Court, what would be the impact on civil rights of possible replacement justices made by President Bush in his second term?

5) Congress also plays a role in civil rights. Do some research to determine what types of civil rights issues Congress has been dealing with in the last four years. What are the separate roles of Congress and the courts in civil rights?

Web Sites

Civil Rights Division, U.S. Department of Justice Web site offers an overview of the activities and programs of the DOJ on civil rights as well as links to documents, legislation, cases, and the Civil Rights Forum Newsletter.

www.usdoj.gov/crt/crt-home.html

U.S. Commission on Civil Rights is a bipartisan, fact-finding agency established within the executive branch. The Web site offers news releases, publications, a calendar of events, and multimedia coverage of civil rights events.
www.usccr.gov/

The **Legal Information Institute** of Cornell University has an excellent site that offers extensive information about the legalities and definitions of civil rights. It begins with a prose definition of a civil right and includes links to U.S. Government laws, state laws, Supreme Court rulings, international laws on civil rights, and more.
www.law.cornell.edu/topics/civil_rights.html

The **National Association for the Advancement of Colored People** (NAACP) Web site offers information about the organization, membership, and issues of interest to proponents of civil rights.
www.naacp.org

The **Southern Poverty Law Center (SPLC)** is a nonprofit group dedicated to fighting hate and intolerance. Their Web site includes information on the center and their activities including a program titled "Teaching Tolerance," the Klanwatch, and Militia Task Force. They also have a state-by-state listing of "hate incidents."
www.splcenter.org

National Organization of Women (NOW) Web site offers information on the organization and its issues/activities, including women in the military, economic equity and reproductive rights. They offer an e-mail action list and the opportunity to join NOW online. Also has links to related sites.
www.now.org

Mexican-American Legal Defense and Education Fund (MALDEF) Web site offers information on scholarships, job opportunities, legal programs, regional offices information, and more.
www.maldef.org

Native American Rights Fund (NARF) Web site offers profiles of issues, an archive, resources, a tribal directory, and treaty information as well as a lot of other information.
www.narf.org

80-20 Initiative is a nonprofit group working to further civil rights for Asian-Americans. Its Web page presents information related to legal and political issues central to the organization's activities.
http://www.80-20.info/

America with Disabilities Act (ADA) offers information on this legislation and rights of the disabled.

www.usdoj.gov/crt/ada/adahoml.htm

EthnicMajority.com is a Web site promoting equal rights and opportunities for African, Latino and Asian Americans. Its page on affirmative action gives an extensive background on the issue and numerous links to organizations promoting and protecting affirmative action.

www.ethnicmajority.com/affirmative_action.htm

Arab American Institute offers a Web page detailing discrimination problems facing Arab American citizens following 9/11.

www.aaiusa.org/discrimination.htm

Anti-Defamation League's Web page on civil rights focuses on several issues, including anti-Semitism.

http://www.adl.org/civil_rights/

The **Legal Information Institute** of Cornell University has an excellent site that offers extensive information about the legalities and definitions of employment discrimination law. It begins with a prose definition of employment law and includes links to U.S. government laws, state laws, Supreme Court rulings, and more.

http://www.law.cornell.edu/topics/employment_discrimination.html

Findlaw is a searchable database of SC decisions plus legal subjects, state courts, law schools, bar associations, and international law.

www.findlaw.com

Practice Tests

MULTIPLE CHOICE QUESTIONS

1)   To resolve the conflict between slave states and nonslave states over the expansion of slavery into new states admitted into the union, Congress, in 1820, passed
   a.   the first Civil Rights Act.
   b.   the Emancipation Proclamation.
   c.   the Missouri Compromise.
   d.   three constitutional amendments known as the Civil War Amendments.

2)   Slavery and involuntary servitude were banned by the _____ Amendment.
   a.   Tenth
   b.   Thirteenth
   c.   Fifteenth
   d.   Seventeenth

3)   Why was the Civil Rights Act of 1866 passed?"

a. to invalidate some Black Codes.

b. to encourage Southern resistance

c. to discourage integration

d. to overturn *Brown v. Board of Education of Topeka, Kansas*

4) The doctrine of "separate but equal" was first enunciated in the case

a. *Dred Scott* v. *Sandford.*

b. *Bradwell* v. *Illinois.*

c. *Minor* v. *Happersett.*

d. *Plessy* v. *Ferguson.*

5) Women were granted the right to vote in 1920 through the _____ Amendment.

a. Fifteenth

b. Seventeenth

c. Nineteenth

d. Twenty-First

6) During the 1930s, the NAACP decided it was time to launch a challenge to the precedent set by *Plessy*. To do so, they used a strategy of

a. litigation.

b. strikes and protests.

c. boycotts.

d. All of the above.

7) The opinion in *Brown* v. *Board of Education* (1954) was written and delivered by

a. Justice Thurgood Marshall.

b. Chief Justice John Marshall.

c. Chief Justice Earl Warren.

d. Justice John Marshall Harlan.

8) In *Brown* v. *Board of Education II* (1955), the Supreme Court ordered that racially segregated public school must be integrated

a. with all deliberate speed.

b. immediately.

c. in the South but not the North.

d. only if civil and political unrest can be avoided in the process.

9) In *Craig* v. *Boren*, the issue at stake was

a. racially segregated public schools.

b. separate but equal facilities.

c. gender discrimination.

d. discrimination against Native Americans.

10) Which group filed suits in Texas and California regarding discriminatory practices against Hispanics?

a. MALDEF
b. NAACP
c. LULAC
d. NARF

11) The civil rights organization founded in 1970 at the same time litigation was being filed by activities trained at the American Indian Law Center at the University of New Mexico was the
a. Lambda Legal Defense Fund.
b. Legal Defense Fund for Women.
c. Native American Rights Fund.
d. Equal Opportunity Employment Commission.

12) In 1996, the Supreme Court ruled for the rights of homosexuals, signaling a change in the public's view toward homosexuality, in the case of
a. *Gregg* v. *Georgia.*
b. *Romer* v. *Evans.*
c. *Furman* v. *Georgia.*
d. *Missouri* v. *Jenkins.*

13) In November of 2003 a state supreme court ruled that denying homosexuals the right to civil marriage was unconstitutional. In what state was that decision made?
a. Massachusetts
b. Colorado
c. California
d. Vermont

14) Disabled people, fueled largely by a group of veterans, won greater protection against discrimination through
a. the Americans with Disabilities Act.
b. the Civil Rights Act of 1964.
c. *Griggs* v. *Duke Power Co.*
d. *Texas* v. *Hopwood.*

15) In 1978, the Supreme Court first addressed the issue of affirmative action in *Regents of the University of California* v. *Bakke.* They ruled that
a. all affirmative action is unconstitutional.
b. race could not be taken into account in admissions decisions.
c. race could be taken into account, but strict quotas were unconstitutional.
d. if affirmative action policies discriminated against a member of the majority who was more qualified, they were unconstitutional.

TRUE/FALSE

1) Black Codes were laws of the Reconstruction South that allowed blacks to vote and exercise their constitutional rights.

2) Some women opposed the Fourteenth Amendment because it failed to guarantee suffrage for women.

3) Poll taxes were used in the South to inhibit African Americans from voting following the adoption of the Fifteenth Amendment.

4) The lone dissenter in *Plessy* v. *Ferguson* (1896), Justice John Marshall Harlan, argued that "the Constitution is colorblind."

5) Women were guaranteed the right to vote in 1920 with the adoption of the Seventeenth Amendment.

6) The Supreme Court's decision in *Brown* v. *Board of Education* overturned its earlier separate-but-equal ruling in *Plessy* v. *Ferguson.*

7) The Montgomery bus boycotts were started by Dr. Martin Luther King, Jr. when he refused to give up his seat on a public bus to a white woman in Montgomery, Alabama, in 1955.

8) The leader of the Southern Senators who opposed the passage of the Civil Rights Act of 1964 was Strom Thurmond of South Carolina, who afterwards switched from the Democratic Party to the Republican Party.

9) The ERA was adopted as the Twenty-Seventh Amendment to the Constitution in 1982.

10) Affirmative action in higher education was ended completely in the 2003 Supreme Court decision *Grutter* v. *Bollinger.*

COMPARE AND CONTRAST

slavery and abolition

African American suffrage movement and the women's suffrage movement

Plessy v. *Ferguson* and *Brown* v. *Board of Education, Topeka, Kansas*

Thirteenth, Fourteenth, Fifteenth Amendments

Black Codes and grandfather clauses

NAACP and NAWSA

Civil Rights Act of 1964 and Civil Rights Act of 1991

suspect classification and strict scrutiny

ESSAY AND SHORT ANSWER QUESTIONS

1) Define civil rights and discuss their constitutional bases.

2) What was the abolitionist movement?

3) Discuss the importance of the Thirteenth, Fourteenth, and Fifteenth Amendments, the Civil War Amendments.

4) Discuss the role the *Brown* decision has had on American society. Has racial equality improved because of it? Was public school desegregation successful in promoting racial equality? Is there more or less segregation in public schools today than 15 years ago?

5) With regard to civil rights, discuss the 2003 Supreme Court case of *Lawrence* v. *Texas* and its significance.

6) Discuss the development of civil rights through from 1800-1890 in American political history.

7) Discuss the history of the women's suffrage and rights movement up to and including the ERA and its ratification drive.

8) The NAACP chose to use a litigation strategy to achieve desegregation and equal rights. How did they implement this strategy, and what were their other choices?

9) Explain the equal protection clause and the constitutional standards of review. Use examples of Supreme Court cases.

10) Once African Americans and women had some success in the battle for equal rights, other groups mobilized to gain their rights. Discuss these groups, the tactics they used, and how successful they have been.

ANSWERS TO STUDY EXERCISES

multiple choice answers

1.	c	p. 168
2.	b	p. 170
3.	a	p. 170
4.	d	p. 173
5.	c	p. 175
6.	a.	p. 176, 180
7.	c	p. 180
8.	a	p. 181
9.	c	p. 187
10.	a	p. 194
11.	c	p. 194
12.	c	p. 195
13.	a.	p. 197
14.	a	p. 197
15.	c	p. 200

true/false answers

1.	F	p. 170
2.	T	p. 170
3.	T	p. 173
4.	T	p. 173
5.	F	p. 175
6.	T	p. 180
7.	F	p. 182
8.	T	p. 184
9.	F	p. 186
10.	F	p. 200

CHAPTER 6
CONGRESS

Chapter Goals and Learning Objectives

Since the first days of our country, a national Congress existed in one form or another. First, the colonies were represented by the Continental Congress, which had little to no authority over the colonies. Then, the states were represented in Congress under the Articles of Confederation, a national legislature that had but a few more powers than before. Article I of the Constitution, however, vested the governing powers of the United States squarely in the hands of "the first branch of government," Congress. Indeed, Congress alone was given the power to create legislation, control the purse, declare war, raise an army, control commerce as well as other national governing authority under Article I, section 8. The United States had no executive branch and, thus, no president under its early government until the adoption of the new Constitution. And even under the new Constitution, the chief executive came in second place (Article II). Despite a balance of powers among the three branches of government, Congress was first among equals.

Today, the president of the United States is first among equals (which will be discussed in the next chapter). Structurally under the Constitution, the powers of Congress have not been diminished. However, few would argue today that the president of the United States stands preeminent over the Congress in many ways. Yet, through much of our history as a nation, the reverse was true: Congress was preeminent over the presidency. Today, the president is, in terms of real and perceived power, the chief policymaker of the country. What has changed over the course of our history regarding Congress? Why can virtually all Americans readily name the president but few can identify their own representatives in Congress?

The Congress of the United States consists of the House of Representatives and the Senate. It enacts our federal laws and sets the federal budget. Members of Congress work to represent their states and districts within their states. Individually, each member of Congress shares power with his or her colleagues. As a body, Congress, the institution, makes laws and policy. Individually, its members work to better the conditions of their states and districts. It is important to understand their duties, how their powers were created, and what their constitutional powers are. This chapter discusses how Congress is organized and how they make laws as a body and how the individual members of Congress make decisions, as well as the relationship between Congress and the executive branch.

This chapter is designed to inform you about the institution of Congress. The main topic headings of the chapter are:

- The Constitution and the Legislative Branch of Government
- How Congress is Organized

- The Members of Congress
- How Members Make Decisions
- The Law-making Function of Congress
- Congress and the President
- Congress and the Judiciary

In each section, there are certain facts and ideas that you should strive to understand. Many are in boldface type and appear in both the narrative and in the glossary at the end of the book. Other ideas, dates, facts, events, people, etc. are more difficult to pull out of the narrative. (Keep in mind that studying for objective-style tests [multiple choice, T/F] is different than studying for essay tests. See the Study Guide section on test taking for hints on study skills.)

In general, after you finish reading and studying this chapter, you should understand the following:

- What the Constitution says about the legislative branch of government
- How Congress is organized
- How members of Congress are elected and what they do
- How members of Congress make decisions
- The law-making function of Congress
- How members of Congress make decisions
- The relationship between Congress and the presidency and its many permutations over our history
- The relationship between Congress and the judicial branch

Chapter Outline and Key Points

In this section, you are provided with a basic outline of the chapter and key words/points you should know. Use this outline to develop a complete outline of the material. Write the definitions or further explanations for the terms. Use the space provided in this workbook or rewrite that material in your notebook. This will help you study and remember the material in preparation for your tests, assignments, and papers.

The Constitution and the Legislative Branch of Government

bicameral legislature—

requirements for membership in the House and Senate—

terms of Representatives and Senators—

how Senators elected under Article I—

Seventeenth Amendment—

Apportionment and Redistricting

size of House in 1790—

House membership set by statute in 1929—

apportionment—

redistricting—

Constitutional Powers of Congress

bill—

Article I, section 8, powers of Congress)—

necessary and proper clause—

Article I structure of Congress (Table 6.1)

key differences between House and Senate (Table 6.2):

constitutional differences—

differences in operation—

changes in the institution—

impeachment process:

role of House—

role of Senate—

advise and consent power of the Senate—

<u>**How Congress is Organized**</u>

a new Congress is seated every _____ years—

hierarchical leadership structure (Figure 6.1)—

The House of Representatives

the first Congress in 1798—

Speaker of the House—

majority party—

[Dennis Hastert, current Speaker]

minority party—

role of Speaker of the House—

Other House Leaders—

party caucus or conference—

majority leader [Tom DeLay]—

minority leader—

Nancy Pelosi—

whip—

The Senate

presiding officer of the Senate and duties—

Constitution specifies vice president of the United States—

not a member of the Senate—

president pro tempore—

majority leader of the Senate and duties—

Bill Frist—

The Role of Parties in Organizing Congress

Congress organized along party lines—

party breakdown for 109th Congress (Figure 6.2)—

what happens at start of new Congress in party caucus or conference?—

Committee on Committees—

Steering Committee—

The Committee System

real legislative work of Congress takes place in committees—

committees especially important in the House—

Committees of the 109th Congress (Table 6.2)—

Republican reorganization of committee structure in 1995—

types of committees:

> standing committees—

> joint committees—

> conference committees—

> select (or special) committees—

House Rules Committee—

discharge petition—

committee membership in the Senate—

Committee Membership—

> importance of committee assignments to members—

> pork—

> committee membership reflects party distribution—

Committee Chairs—

> role of chairs—

> seniority—

selection of chairs in the House—

The Members of Congress

some reasons why members of Congress do not seek reelection—

constituencies that members of Congress must attempt to appease—

A Day in the Life of a Member of Congress (Table 6.3)—

Running for Office and Staying in Office

how many members of Congress?—

membership in political party—

incumbency—

approval ratings of Congress and district representatives—

in 2004, what percentage of incumbents won reelection?—

Congressional Demographics

general demographics of members of Congress—

Theories of Representation

trustee—

delegate—

politico—

How Members Make Decisions

Party

looking to party leaders—

reign of partisanship—

divided government—

both Congress and presidency controlled by what party?—

reasons members vote the way they do relative to party membership—

Constituents

constituents—

how often do members vote in conformity with people in the districts?—

Colleagues and Caucuses

when do members turn to colleagues about a vote?—

logrolling—

special-interest caucuses—

Interest Groups, Lobbyists, and Political Action Committees

primary functions of most lobbyists—

campaign contributions and high cost of campaigning—

grassroots appeals—

Staff and Support Agencies

members reliance on staff—

duties of staff—

committee staff—

Congressional Research Service and other congressional support offices—

The Law-making Function of Congress

who can formally submit a bill for congressional consideration—

approximately number of bills introduced in each Congress and how many become law—

How a Bill Becomes a Law

How a Bill Becomes a Law (Figure 6.4)—

the three stages a bill must survive before it becomes law:

1)

2)

3)

role of committee and subcommittee—

House Rules Committee—

Committee of the Whole—

hold—

filibusters—

cloture—

when two chambers of Congress approve different versions of same bill—

conference committee (a bill must pass both houses in the same language to go to the president)

veto—

four options of president regarding veto—

pocket veto—

Congress and the President

the relationship before and after the 1930s—

The Shifting Balance of Power

why Congress now responds to executive branch proposals—

Congressional Oversight of the Executive Branch

oversight—

key to Congress's performance of its oversight function—

purpose of hearings—

congressional review—

Foreign Affairs Oversight—

> separate constitution role of Congress and the president in foreign policy—

> War Powers Act of 1973—

Confirmation of Presidential Appointments—

> Condoleezza Rice—

> role of Senate—

> senatorial courtesy—

Impeachment Process—

> *Federalist No. 65*—

> The Eight Stages of the Impeachment Process (Table 6.4)—

Congress and the Judiciary

> ways in which Congress can exercise control over the federal judiciary—

> setting jurisdiction of federal courts—

> actions by Congress in 2004 in response to federal court decisions—

Research Ideas and Possible Paper Topics

1) Do some research and compare how different or similar the 108th Congress is to the 109th in terms of party majority, leadership, representation, minorities, women, structure, incumbency advantage, and rules. What accounts for the similarities and differences?

2) Using the Congressional Web site or government documents, research the transition between the 108th and 109th Congresses. What happened from election day 2004 to office-taking in January 2005? How are new members introduced to the rules, protocols, and traditions of the House and Senate? What happens to staff if their member is defeated? How do new members recruit staff? How are leaders chosen? How are rules made? Are there any "left-over issues" from the 108th? What impact has the 109th Congress had on the country?

3) Pick a piece of legislation from the current session of Congress. Write a legislative history of that bill or law. Outline the steps it took, who supported it, who opposed it, and various other influences on its passage. Were there hearings? witnesses? controversy? Does this compare with what you learned in the text about the law-making process? How?

4) Most Americans claim to dislike and distrust Congress but like and trust their own member of Congress. What explains this paradox? Do some research on public opinion and voting behavior, analyze the media coverage of Congress, think about what members of Congress do, and why this would be the case. Prepare a presentation explaining this phenomenon for class. See if you can determine how your own U.S. Representative is perceived in your area as well.

5) There have been a number of high-profile scandals in the Congress throughout history. Americans now seem quite concerned about the ethics of the legislature. Do some research on scandals in Congress. How many have there been? How severe have they been? How widespread have they been? Is it a few bad apples or the whole barrel? Be sure to look at how the media have covered these scandals and the lack thereof in your discussion of the ethical nature of Congress.

Web Sites

Thomas is the official government Web site about the United States Congress from the **Library of Congress** with information on legislation, the *Congressional Record*, as well as numerous links to Congress-related sites.
> http://thomas.loc.gov

Official site of the **U.S. House of Representatives**.
> http://www.house.gov

Official site of the **U.S. Senate**.
> www.Senate.gov

YourCongress.com is an expansive, easily accessible Web site about Congress, its members, its issues, its lobbyists, and how you can influence it. The site states that it "combines irreverent articles, behind-the-scenes information, and the revolutionary Congress. Watch tracking services to give everyone an easy and entertaining way to find out what's going on in Congress."
> http://www.yourcongress.com

C-SPAN provides the most extensive coverage of Congress available on television over its three cable channels. Its Web site allows you to follow congressional action as it is broadcast on C-SPAN with streaming video or audio. The Web site is sponsored by C-

SPAN and Congressional Quarterly and has headings such as Write to Congress, Directory of Congress, Vote Library, Capital Questions, Live Hearings and many more.
www.c-span.org/capitolspotlight/index.asp

Congressional Quarterly is a nonpartisan publication whose mission is to inform the electorate. Site includes information on Congress including bios, votes, election information, and so on. They also have a link to their state and local level publication.
www.cq.com/

GPO Access by the U.S. Government Printing Office offers the full text of many federal government publications on the Web, including the Congressional Record. Among the growing list of titles available are the Federal Register, Congressional Bills, United States Code, Economic Indicators and GAO Reports.
http://www.gpoaccess.gov/legislative.html

The Hill: The Capital Newspaper. "The Hill reports and analyzes the actions of Congress as it struggles to reconcile the needs of those it represents with the legitimate needs of the administration, lobbyists, and the news media. We explain the pressures confronting policymakers, and the many ways—often unpredictable—that decisions are made. But Capitol Hill is more than the focal point of the legislative branch of government. It is also a community not unlike a small city, and we report on its culture, social life, crime, employment, traffic, education, discrimination, shopping, dining, travel, and recreation. Our editorial viewpoint is nonpartisan and nonideological." Published on Wednesdays.
www.hillnews.com

RollCall On-Line. "Roll Call is widely regarded as the leading source for Congressional news and information both inside the Beltway and beyond." RollCall On-Line publishes many of the same stories, classifieds, etc. that the print edition publishes. Published on Mondays and Thursdays.
www.rollcall.com

Congress.Org is a joint venture of two Washington, D.C. area firms with expertise in communicating with Congress. Capitol Advantage and Issue Dynamics (IDI) teamed up to produce Congress.Org in 1996. Some search engines refer to it as a "one-stop shop" for legislative information including contact information on members, committee assignments, etc.
www.congress.org

Public Citizens' Congress Watch is a consumer interest group that monitors and lobbies Congress. Its Web page reports on its actions and issues in the current Congress.
http://www.citizen.org/congress

The Washington Post. Check out the "Today in Congress" section, including committee hearings and votes. Also click "OnPolitics" for the latest in-depth political news of Congress.

Project Vote-Smart is a nonpartisan information service funded by members and nonpartisan foundations. It offers "a wealth of facts on your political leaders, including biographies and addresses, issue positions, voting records, campaign finances, evaluations by special interests." It also offers "CongressTrack," a way for citizens to track the status of legislation, members and committees, sponsors, voting records, clear descriptions, full text, and weekly floor schedules, as well as access to information on elections, federal and state governments, the issues, and politics. Includes thousands of links to the most important sites on the Internet.

www.vote-smart.org/

Practice Tests

MULTIPLE CHOICE QUESTIONS

1) Which of the following is correct about the terms of members of Congress?
   a. Senators serve four-year terms, and House members serve two-year terms.
   b. Senators serve six-year terms, and House members serve two-year terms.
   c. Senators serve six-year terms, and House members serve four-year terms.
   d. Both Senators and House members serve two year terms.

2) The Senate was originally chosen by state legislators. This was changed to direct election in 1913 with the passage of the _____ Amendment.
   a. Seventeenth
   b. Eighteenth
   c. Nineteenth
   d. Twentieth

3) Every ten years, seats in the U.S. House of Representatives are apportioned to reflect population changes and shifts among the states following the report of the
   a. House Rules Committee.
   b. President's Commission of House Reapportionment.
   c. U.S. Census.
   d. Senate Appropriations Committee.

4) The clause of the Constitution that has allowed Congress to expand its powers without constitutional amendment is called the
   a. supremacy clause.
   b. necessary and proper clause.
   c. full faith and credit clause.
   d. privileges and immunities clause.

5) Revenue bills are introduced by
   a. only the president.

b.   the House or Senate.
c.   only the Senate.
d.   only the House.

6)   A main difference between the House and the Senate is that
a.   House members are highly specialized.
b.   the operation of Senate is less centralized and less formal.
c.   the House has a Rules Committee.
d.   All of the above.

7)   The only House officer specifically mentioned in the Constitution is the
a.   president pro tempore.
b.   majority leader of the Senate.
c.   speaker of the house.
d.   sergeant at arms.

8)   The House Minority Leader in the 109th Congress is
a.   Dennis Hastert.
b.   Tom DeLay.
c.   Newt Gingrich.
d.   Nancy Pelosi.

9)   The presiding officer of the Senate, according to the Constitution, is the
a.   vice president of the United States.
b.   president pro tempore of the Senate.
c.   majority leader of the Senate.
d.   speaker.

10)   The true leader of the Senate is
a.   vice president of the United States.
b.   president pro tempore.
c.   majority leader.
d.   speaker.

11)   The House committee, which reviews most bills after they come from committee
and before they go to the full House for consideration, is called
a.   a joint committee.
b.   the Governmental Affairs Committee.
c.   the Rules Committee.
d.   the Ways and Means Committee.

12)   Approximately _____ bills are introduced in each session of Congress.
a.   500
b.   4,000
c.   7,500
d.   9,000

13) A tactic by which a senator asks to be informed before a particular bill is brought to the floor, in effect stopping the bill temporarily, is called a
   a. discharge petition.
   b. cloture.
   c. block.
   d. hold.

14) Since the 1960s, there has been a substantial increase in the use of one of Congress's functions in which it questions members of the president's administration on issues pertaining to execution of congressional directives. That function is called
   a. law-making.
   b. oversight.
   c. impeachment and removal.
   d. advise and consent.

15) The War Powers Act was passed by Congress over the president's veto in reaction to presidential expansion of military powers during the
   a. Vietnam War.
   b. second World War.
   c. first Gulf War.
   d. second invasion of Iraq.

TRUE/FALSE QUESTIONS

1) In 1929, the size of the House of Representatives was fixed at 435 by statute.

2) The House of Representatives has the authority to approve presidential appointments.

3) The Senate Rules Committee is very powerful and controls the flow of legislation in the Senate.

4) Every two years, a new Congress is seated.

5) The speaker is traditionally a member of the majority party in the House.

6) The Constitution specifies that the presiding officer of the Senate is the Senate majority leader.

7) Much of the actual legislative work of Congress is done within the committee system.

8) Increasing partisanship in Congress has played a role in a number of recent retirements from that body.

9) Any governmental official may introduce a bill for the consideration of Congress.

10) Congress has the power to establish the size of the U.S. Supreme Court.

COMPARE AND CONTRAST

bill and law

impeachment and removal

differences in operation between the House and Senate

powers of House and Senate

officers of House and Senate

trustees, delegates, and politicos

standing committees, ad hoc committees, joint committees, and conference committees

rules in the House and the Senate on speaking about issues and bills

general veto, line-item veto, and legislative veto

SHORT ANSWER AND ESSAY QUESTIONS

1) Discuss the history of the legislative branch prior to the adoption of the U.S. Constitution.

2) What are apportionment and redistricting and their implications?

3) Discuss the incumbency advantage for members of Congress.

4) How representative is Congress? (Be sure to discuss the definition and theories of representation.)

5) Discuss the types of committees in Congress.

6) What are the constitutional powers of Congress?

7) How do the powers and functions of the House and Senate differ?

8) Discuss the role of political parties in the House and Senate.

9) What is the law-making function of Congress? Compare and contrast the two ways the text discusses about how a bill becomes a law. Be sure to specify all points at which a bill could die.

10) How do members of Congress make decisions?

ANSWERS TO STUDY EXERCISES

multiple choice answers

1.	b	p. 205
2.	a	p. 205
3.	c.	p. 206
4.	b	p. 206
5.	d	p. 208
6.	d	p. 208
7.	c	p. 210
8.	d	p. 211
9.	a	p. 211
10.	c	p. 215
11.	c	p. 218
12.	d	p. 230
13.	d	p. 232
14.	b	p. 234
15.	a	p. 235

true/false answers

1.	T	p. 206
2.	F	p. 208
3.	F	p. 208
4.	T	p. 208
5.	T	p. 210
6.	F	p. 215
7.	T	p. 217
8.	T	p. 221
9.	F	p. 230
10.	T	p. 237

CHAPTER 7
THE PRESIDENCY

Chapter Goals and Learning Objectives

Ask a friend, "Who is your Congressman?" and you'll likely get a blank stare in return. Ask her, however, "Who is the president?" and she will respond instantly, "George Bush, of course!" As the Framers designed our constitutional government, Congress was the first branch of government, but in the modern era it has taken a back seat in American politics to the president, not only in public awareness but in raw power. The constitutional authority, statutory powers, and burdens of the modern presidency make it a powerful position and an awesome responsibility. Most of the men who have been president in the past two decades have done their best; yet, in the heightened expectations of the American electorate, most have come up short. Our awareness of the president in our public life is high, and our expectations of the man in that office are even higher. Not only did the Framers not envision such a powerful role for the president, they could not have foreseen the skepticism with which many presidential actions are now greeted in the press, on talk radio, and on the Internet. These expectations have also led presidents into policy areas never dreamed of by the Framers.

This chapter is designed to give you a basic understanding of the presidency as an institution as well as some information on the men who have occupied the office. The main topic headings of the chapter are:

- The Roots and Rules Governing the Office of President of the United States
- The Constitutional Powers of the President
- The Development and Expansion of Presidential Power
- The Presidential Establishment
- The President as Policy Maker
- Presidential Leadership and the Importance of Public Opinion

In each section, you will find certain facts and ideas that you should work to understand. Many are in boldface type and appear in both the narrative and in the glossary at the end of the book. Other ideas, dates, facts, events, people, etc. are more difficult to find in the narrative. (Keep in mind that the process of reading and studying for objective exams [multiple choice, T/F] is different than for essay tests. See the Study Guide section on test taking for help with study skills.)

In general, after you finish reading and studying this chapter, you should understand the following:

- the roots of the office of president of the United States and how the Framers created the executive for a new nation
- Article II and the constitutional powers of the presidency
- The development and expansion of presidential power and how presidential success has come to depend on the officeholder's personality, popularity, and leadership style
- The growth of the presidential establishment of advisors, assistants, and departments, all helping the president do his job, but making it easier for him to lose touch with the people
- The president as maker of policy
- Presidential leadership and the significance of public opinion as well as the role the president plays in molding public opinion

---

Chapter Outline and Key Points

In this section, you are provided with a basic outline of the chapter and key words/points you should know. Use this outline to develop a complete outline of the material. Write the definitions or further explanations for the terms. Use the space provided in this workbook or rewrite that material in your notebook. This will help you study and remember the material in preparation for your tests, assignments, and papers.

The Roots of and Rules Governing the Office of President of the United States

no executive branch under the Articles of Confederation, thus, no president of the United States under the Articles of Confederation—

George Washington, first president, under Constitution of the United States—

Presidential Qualifications and Terms of Office

qualifications—

term limit under Article II of Constitution—

Franklin D. Roosevelt—

Twenty-Second Amendment—

office of vice-president—

Removal from Office

impeachment—

separate roles of House and Senate in impeachment process—

only president to resign—

Watergate—

executive privilege—

U.S. v. *Nixon* (1974)—

Rules of Succession

number of presidents to have died in office—

constitutional line of succession—

Presidential Succession Act of 1947—

Twenty-Fifth Amendment—

Gerald R. Ford—

Spiro T. Agnew—

Nelson A. Rockefeller—

<u>The Constitutional Powers of the President</u>

Article II—

first sentence of Article II—

The Appointment Power

appointment of ambassadors, federal judges, executive positions—

president's appointments to his administration—

how president sets the policy agenda—

Cabinet—

The Power to Convene Congress

"State of the Union"—

"extraordinary Occasions"—

power to convene Congress only symbolic significance now (why?)—

The Power to Make Treaties

"receive ambassadors"—

advise and consent of the Senate—

Jimmy Carter and Panama Canal Treaty—

executive agreement—

Veto Power

exception to veto power—

veto power—

Madison's argument in Constitutional Convention—

congressional override—

how many presidential vetoes and how many overridden—

The Power to Preside over the Military as Commander in Chief

"Commander in Chief"—

Lincoln's use of commander in chief clause—

War Powers Act—

Gulf of Tonkin Resolution—

George W. Bush and Iraq war—

The Pardoning Power

pardon—

Gerald Ford and Richard Nixon—

The Development and Expansion of Presidential Power

John F. Kennedy and Harry S Truman on the presidency—

Lincoln and the presidency—

limits on presidential powers—

factors influencing a president's use of his powers—

inherent powers—

Best and Worse Presidents (Table 7.3)—

The Growth of the Modern Presidency

before broadcast communications, balance of power weighed heavily in favor of Congress—

trend of importance in decision making shifting from Congress to President began with Franklin D. Roosevelt (FDR)—

FDR's handling of the Great Depression—

FDR's New Deal program—

FDR's unprecedented four elective terms—

how FDR personalized the presidency for the American people—

fireside chats—

FDR and the modern presidency—

The Presidential Establishment

The Vice President

to balance the ticket—

John Nance Garner on the vice presidency—

Walter Mondale—

Dick Cheney—

Al Gore—

The Cabinet

Cabinet—

no provision for Cabinet in Constitution—

Cabinet Departments—

The U.S. Cabinet and Responsibilities of Each Executive Department (Table 7.4)—

The First Lady

when the term "first lady" was coined—

role of first lady—

Laura Bush—

themes of Smithsonian exhibition on first ladies—

The Executive Office of the President (EOP)

The Executive Office of the President—

National Security Council (NSC)—

Office of Faith-Based and Community Initiatives—

The White House Staff

personal assistants to the president—

Executive Office Building—

importance of proximity to Oval Office—

<u>The President as Policy Maker</u>

FDR claimed leadership role for presidency in the legislative process—

The President's Role in Proposing and Facilitation Legislation

from FDR's presidency to the Republican-controlled 104th Congress, public looked to president to set legislative agenda—

Contract with America and presumed reassertion of congressional power—

Bill Clinton's continued forceful presence in budgetary process making Congress's resurgent role largely illusory—

presidents have hard time getting Congress to pass programs—

when presidents are most likely to win—

honeymoon period and its importance—

patronage—

Tip O'Neill and the Carter White House—

president's use of political party loyalty—

The Budgetary Process and Legislative Implementation

importance of budget process for the president—

FDR and the Bureau of the Budget (1939)—

Office of Management and Budget (OMB)—

Policy-Making Through Regulation

executive order—

Truman ended segregation in the military—

LBJ institutionalized affirmative action as national policy—

use by Reagan, Clinton and Bush of executive orders—

Presidential Leadership and the Importance of Public Opinion

Presidential Leadership

Presidential Personalities (Table 7.5)—

examples of how "great crises make great presidents"—

significance of a president's ability to grasp the importance of leadership style—

how George W. Bush used September 11, 2001, to change public perception of his leadership—

Presidential Personality and the Power to Persuade

key to a president amassing greater power and authority—

Richard Neustadt—

power to persuade—

why persuasion is key—

Going Public: Mobilizing Public Opinion

bully pulpit—

"going public"—

The Public's Perception of Presidential Performance

cyclical pattern of presidential popularity—

Bill Clinton ended presidency with higher approval rating than any president in recent history—

George W. Bush rallying point due to foreign events—

Research Ideas and Possible Paper Topics

1) Examine the growth and impact of the modern presidency. Compare it to the role of the president through the first century-and-a-half of the history of the United States. What precipitated the development of the modern presidency, and what fueled its tremendous development over the past 70 years? Discuss what you think James Madison and Alexander Hamilton might say about the modern status of the limited chief executive they helped create.

2) Do some research on the vice presidency of Dick Cheney. How does his role compare and contrast with other recent vice presidents? What types of activities

has he been involved in and why? Is it a function of his personal relationship with Bush or a permanent change in the office of the vice president? What role, if any, did 9/11 and the invasion of Iraq have in Cheney's role? Discuss.

3)   We have experienced periods of "divided government" where the Congress is of one party and the presidency of another. The executive and legislative branches have also recently been controlled by one party. Do some research into public opinion on this issue. Which situation do Americans prefer? Why? Also research the impact divided government has had on the policy process versus the impact of single-party control. Do more bills fail in a divided government? Are Congress and the president more confrontational due to partisan differences in a divided government? Which scenario works better for our democracy? Discuss.

4)   Choose two presidents from history and write a paper discussing the impact they had on the office. Two interesting variants might be to choose one president who had a positive effect and one who had a negative effect, or to choose two extremely different personalities who seem equally successful and explain why.

5)   Group Project: Do an analysis of the media's coverage of President Bush during his second term. For one month, watch a variety of network and cable news programs, read a variety of newspapers and weekly news magazines, listen to talk radio (be sure to get right- and left-wing programs), and check out Internet news sites. How is the president covered? What gets the attention of the media and why? Is the president "staging" or "spinning" any of the coverage or are the media in control? Also look at how the president is portrayed in entertainment programming. What implications do your findings have on how we perceive the president?

Web Sites

The official **White House** site for information on George W. Bush and the office of the president.
http://www.whitehouse.gov

The **National Archives and Records Administration** offers links to all presidential libraries.
http://www.archives.gov/presidential_libraries/addresses/addresses.html

The **National Portrait Gallery's Hall of Presidents** has information on and portraits of American presidents.
http://www.npg.si.edu/collect/hall.htm

The **University of North Carolina** site offers biographies of the presidents and first ladies, including links to presidential libraries.
http://www.ibiblio.org/lia/president

Federal Web Locator has links to all government Web sites, including presidential sites.
www.infoctr.edu/fwl

The Atlantic Monthly offers a simulation of presidential decision making. Several scenarios from 1996 to 2000 were offered in the magazine and are archived on their Web site. Advisory memos are presented by policy advisors. The reader is then asked to make a decision. After submitting a decision, readers could provide interactive feedback about the effects of the decision. Entertaining but useful tool to demonstrate the politics of decision making and why the "best" decisions are not always the political ones.
http://www.theatlantic.com/politics/decision/memos.htm

POTUS: Presidents of the United States is assembled by the Internet Public Library and provides background information, election results, Cabinet members, notable events, and some points of interest on each of the presidents. Links to biographies, historical documents, audio and video files, and other presidential sites listed.
http://www.ipl.org/div/potus/

You can search the **Public Papers of the Presidents of the United States** online at this site provided by the Office of the Federal Registrar. Not all presidential papers are available currently online. Presidential photographs can be accessed as well.
http://www.access.gpo.gov/nara/pubpaps/srchpaps.html

Statistics, facts, and biographies of U.S. vice presidents are available at **Vice-Presidents.Com**.
http://www.vicepresidents.com/

Current events and video clips about the Bush Administration are available on the **C-SPAN** Web site page devoted to the Executive Branch. Use the URL below, then click on "Bush Administration" link under "Featured Topics" on top left of page.
http://www.c-span.org/

Practice Tests

MULTIPLE CHOICE QUESTIONS

1) In order to be president of the United States, according to the Constitution, a candidate must be
   a. male.
   b. at least 45 years old.
   c. a resident for over five years.
   d. a natural-born citizen

2) Article II of the Constitution says the president
   a. may serve only two terms.

b.   is limited to a maximum of ten years in office.
c.   serves a four-year term.
d.   serves a six-year term.

3)   The Presidential Succession Act of 1947 states that if the president should die and the vice president cannot succeed him, then the next in line is the
a.   speaker of the house.
b.   president pro tempore of the Senate.
c.   secretary of state.
d.   majority leader of the Senate.

4)   The first president to assume that office after appointment, not election, to the office of the vice presidency was

a.   William H. Harrison.
b.   Dwight D. Eisenhower.
c.   Gerald R. Ford.
d.   George Bush.

5)   Which of the following offices is the president not constitutionally empowered to appoint?
a.   members of the U.S. Supreme Court
b.   U.S. ambassadors to foreign countries
c.   officers of the United States (such as Cabinet officers)
d.   speakers of the House and presidents pro tempore of the Senate

6)   The president can enter into treaty-like relations with foreign countries for his term without Senate approval on the basis of
a.   executive powers.
b.   executive privilege.
c.   executive orders.
d.   executive agreements.

7)   The president is authorized to act as commander in chief of U.S. military forces under the authority vested in him by
a.   Congress under the Article I, Section 8 power "to declare war."
b.   the War Powers Act of 1973.
c.   Article II of the Constitution.
d.   the decision of the Supreme Court in *United States* v. *Nixon.*

8)   Richard Nixon was pardoned "for any offenses against the United States, which he…has committed or may have committed while in office" by
a.   the U.S. Supreme Court.
b.   President Lyndon B. Johnson.
c.   President Gerald R. Ford.
d.   President Jimmy Carter.

9)   Lincoln has been cited as perhaps the greatest president due in large part to his strong leadership during the
       a.   Revolutionary War.
       b.   War of 1812.
       c.   Civil War.
       d.   Spanish-American War.

10)   For much of the nation's history, particularly before the advent of electronic communications, which branch of government made most decisions and was closest to the American people?
       a.   legislative branch
       b.   executive branch
       c.   judicial branch
       d.   olive branch

11)   The growth of the modern presidency began with
       a.   Thomas Jefferson.
       b.   Abraham Lincoln.
       c.   Franklin D. Roosevelt.
       d.   Ronald Reagan.

12)   The last Cabinet department established in 2002 is the Department of
       a.   Homeland Security
       b.   Energy.
       c.   Veteran's Affairs.
       d.   Education.

13)   The Executive Office of the President was established by
       a.   Abraham Lincoln.
       b.   Franklin D. Roosevelt.
       c.   Lyndon B. Johnson.
       d.   Ronald Reagan.

14)   According to Richard Neustadt, the most important presidential power is
       a.   his constitutional power.
       b.   the mandate power.
       c.   the power to persuade.
       d.   his commander in chief power.

15)   The term "bully pulpit" was used first by what president to describe the power of the president to reach out to the American people to gain support for his programs?
       a.   Theodore Roosevelt
       b.   Woodrow Wilson
       c.   Franklin D. Roosevelt
       d.   John F. Kennedy

TRUE/FALSE QUESTIONS

1)   Under the Articles of Confederation, no executive branch, and therefore no president, existed.

2)   The president is limited to two terms in Article II of the Constitution.

3)   In 1967, the Twenty-Fifth Amendment was added to the Constitution to allow a president to nominate a replacement to fill a vacancy.

4)   The first use of the Twenty-Fifth Amendment was when Gerald R. Ford appointed Nelson Rockefeller to be his vice president.

5)   Article II gives the president power to appoint members of his Cabinet, with the approval of the Senate.

6)   The president's power to make treaties is limited by the requirement of a vote of two-thirds of the Senate to ratify the treaty.

7)   The Senate can override a presidential veto with a simple majority vote.

8)   While only the Congress has the power to declare war, the president has the power to make and wage war.

9)   Since the 1973 adoption of the War Powers Act by Congress, each president since Richard Nixon agreed that the War Powers Act is a constitutionally permissible limit on his executive power.

10)   Direct, personal appeals to the American people by the president, going over the heads of Congress via radio and television (called "going public") effectively empowers the president to influence Congress.

COMPARE AND CONTRAST

executive agreement and executive order

general and line-item veto

presidential and congressional war powers

the Cabinet and the EOP

presidential and congressional roles in the budget-making process the Article II presidency versus the modern presidency

ESSAY AND SHORT ANSWER QUESTIONS

1) What are the formal requirements for the presidency? Are there also informal requirements? What are they?

2) How is the vice president chosen, and what are the duties of the office? Have they changed over time? Why?

3) How did the first three presidents affect the powers of the presidency?

4) Compare and contrast the nature and functions of the Cabinet, the Executive Office of the President, and other advisors.

5) Discuss the nature of war powers. What are the presidential and congressional powers at issue and has this conflict been solved?

6) Discuss the roots of the office of president and the constitutional debate surrounding the office of the presidency, including a full discussion of the results: Article II.

7) How has presidential power developed? What makes for a powerful president?

8) Analyze the nature and functions of the "presidential establishment."

9) What is the role of the president in the legislative process? What makes a president most effective in this role?

10) Discuss why Americans are dissatisfied with the office of the presidency and whomever inhabits it. What proposals have been made to reform the presidency? Do they adequately reflect the problems and conflicts of the office? Can we "fix" the presidency so that the majority of Americans are satisfied? Discuss.

ANSWERS TO STUDY EXERCISES

multiple choice answers

1.	d	p. 243
2.	c	p. 243
3.	a	p. 244
4.	c	p. 245
5.	b	p. 246
6.	d	p. 247

7.	c	p. 248, 249
8.	c	p. 249
9.	c	p. 254
10.	a	p. 254
11.	c	p. 254, 255
12.	a	p. 257
13.	b	p. 258
14.	c	p. 266
15.	a	p. 266

true/false answers

1.	T	p. 242
2.	F	p. 243
3.	T	p. 244
4.	F	p. 245
5.	T	p. 246
6.	T	p. 247
7.	F	p. 248
8.	T	p. 248, 249
9.	T	p. 249
10.	T	p. 266

CHAPTER 8
THE EXECUTIVE BRANCH AND THE FEDERAL BUREAUCRACY

Chapter Goals and Learning Objectives

Often called the "fourth branch of government" because of the power agencies and bureaus can exercise, the federal bureaucracy draws criticism from many sectors. Political conservatives charge that the bureaucracy is too liberal and that its functions constitute unnecessary government inference in the business sector. In contrast, liberals view the bureaucracy as too slow, too unimaginative to solve America's problems, and too zealous a guardian of the status quo. And while many Americans complain of the efficiency and impact of the government, most Americans regard the government services they receive through the bureaucracy important to their lives. Indeed, it is the executive branch organizations that deliver the myriad of services citizens have come to expect from their government. A basic knowledge of these organizations is important to you, a consumer of these services.

This chapter is designed to give you a better understanding of the executive branch and federal bureaucracy. The main topic headings of this chapter are:

- The Executive Branch and the Development of the Federal Bureaucracy
- The Modern Bureaucracy
- How the Bureaucracy Works
- Holding Agencies Accountable

In each section, there are certain facts and ideas that you should strive to understand. Many are in boldface type and appear in both the narrative and in the glossary at the end of the book. Other ideas, dates, facts, events, people, etc. are more difficult to pull out of the narrative. (Keep in mind that studying for objective-style tests [multiple choice, T/F] is different than studying for essay tests. See the Study Guide section on test taking for hints on study skills.)

In general, after you finish reading and studying this chapter, you should understand the following:

- The development of the federal bureaucracy in the executive branch
- The modern bureaucracy is structured by examining its formal organization and those who work in it
- How the bureaucracy works
- How to make executive branch agencies accountable

In this section, you are provided with a basic outline of the chapter and key words/points you should know. Use this outline to develop a complete outline of the material. Write the definitions or further explanations for the terms. Use the space provided in this workbook or rewrite that material in your notebook. This will help you study and remember the material in preparation for your tests, assignments, and papers.

bureaucracy—

The Executive Branch and the Development of the Federal Bureaucracy

characteristics of model bureaucracies—
1)
2)
3)
4)
5)
6)

Bureaucracy in the United States

the number of civilian employees directly employed in the executive branch—

the number of military employees in the Department of Defense—

the number of employees of the Postal Service (which is a quasi-governmental corporation and not part of the executive branch)—

the three executive branch departments in 1789—

subsequent executive offices under George Washington—

The Civil War and the Growth of Government

the Civil War and the federal bureaucracy—

Pension Office—

From Spoils System to the Merit System

spoils system—

patronage—

Pendleton Act—

civil service system—

merit system—

Regulating the Economy and the Growth of Government in the Twentieth Century

Interstate Commerce Commission—

independent regulatory commissions—

Sixteenth Amendment—

federal reaction to Great Depression—

expansion of federal bureaucracy due to World War II—

the civil rights movement and President Lyndon B. Johnson—

Government Workers and Political Involvement

Hatch Act—

Federal Employees Political Activities Act of 1993—

The Modern Bureaucracy

ways in which the national government differs from private business—

how public sector employees view risks and rewards—

Who Are Bureaucrats?

federal bureaucrats—

General Schedule (GS)—

protection from being fired for political reasons—

competitive examinations—

types of federal government jobs—

federal jobs not covered by the civil service system—

Number of Federal Employees in the Executive Branch, 1789-2002—

job skills represented in the federal workforce—

graying of the federal workforce—

Formal Organization

areas of specialization—

department—

Cabinet Departments—

Cabinet secretaries—

Executive Branch (Figure 8.3)—

what features departments share—

Government Corporations—

Independent Executive Agencies—

Independent Regulatory Commissions—

selecting members of boards and commissions—

<u>How the Bureaucracy Works</u>

congressional delegation of Article I, section 8, powers—

implementation—

iron triangles—

issue networks—

interagency councils—

policy coordinating committees—

Making Policy

administrative discretion—

Rule making—

regulations---

Administrative Procedures Act of 1946 rule-making procedures:

1)

2)

3)

Administrative adjudication—

quasi-judicial—

administrative law judges—

Making Agencies Accountable

Executive Control

president has what authority?—

executive order—

Congressional Control

Congress has what authority?—

investigatory powers—

power of the purse—

Congressional review, adopted by 104th Congress—

Judicial Control

federal judiciary has what authority?—

injunctions—

courts usually defer to bureaucrats—

specialized courts—

Research Ideas and Possible Paper Topics

1) Service Learning (learn by doing): Visit at least three federal offices in your area. Research each agency on the Internet prior to your visit. Watch what goes on. Ask questions. Investigate the functions and efficiencies of the procedures used. If possible, schedule interviews with managers and staff at these offices. Ask about misconceptions and problems with the bureaucracy. How does what you find compare with what you learned in the text?

2) One of the oldest bureaucratic departments is the Department of State. Research to determine how they have reorganized over the years to cope with new challenges and directives. How large is the DOS? What functions do they perform? What is their budget? How effective are they in carrying out their goals? In addition, analyze whether the current Secretary of State has managed to change the culture of the department, and if so, how?

3) The postal service has changed its relationship with the government and the American people over time. Research the history of the postal service, its past and present ties to the government, its effectiveness, and reputation. Many of us complain incessantly about the mail. Are we justified? How are rate increases determined? If we are truly unhappy, what avenues of complaint are open?

4) Service Learning (learn by doing): Write to or visit your local congressional office. Ask to speak with one of the caseworkers who deals with bureaucratic snafus and red tape. Find out how they intervene on behalf of constituents, how effective they are, how many constituents avail themselves of this service, and their impressions of the bureaucracy. Write a paper or discuss in class what you have learned.

5) How does the bureaucracy affect you? Consider the innumerable ways that government helps or hinders your life. Keep a journal for the semester and note in it ways you interact with bureaucracy and government. At the end of class, compare notes with friends and colleagues. Discuss whether, in total, your experiences with government are positive, negative, or neutral.

Web Sites

President Bush's Cabinet is a Web site hosted by the White House presenting photographs of Cabinet officers and biographies. You can go to each of the individual departments via links for each on this Web site.

Federal Web Locator provided by the Chicago-Kent College of Law has links to all government Web sites, including all governmental departments, agencies, corporations, and affiliates.

      www.infoctr.edu/fwl

FedWorld, hosted by the Department of Commerce, is a comprehensive index of federal government agencies, searchable by keyword. Access to thousands of U.S. government Web sites, more than a 1/2 million U.S. government documents, databases, and other information products with links to the FedWorld File Libraries and other sources.

      www.fedworld.gov

GovExec.com is online version of a magazine for federal employees called **Government Executive.** The Web site offers breaking news stories, analysis, and information about the federal community

      www.govexec.com

The Washington Post reports on the activities of the federal bureaucracy for an audience keenly interested in news about it—Washington-based employees of the federal government—in a section entitled **Federal Page**. (Free registration is required for access to the Washington Post.)

      http://www.washingtonpost.com/wp-dyn/politics/fedpage

Practice Tests

MULTIPLE CHOICE QUESTIONS

1) In 2005, the executive branch had approximately ___ million nonpostal, civilian employees.
    a.   1.8
    b.   2.6
    c.   3.9
    d.   6.9

2) The reform measure that created the merit-based civil service is commonly referred to as the
    a.   Anti-Patronage Act.
    b.   Hatch Act.
    c.   Pendleton Act.
    d.   Garfield Act.

3) The first independent regulatory commission, established to regulate railroad rates after the Civil War, was called the
    a.   Independent Transportation Commission.

b. Federal Trade Commission.
c. National Railroad Relations Board.
d. Interstate Commerce Commission.

4) Hundreds of new federal agencies were created to regulate business practices and various aspects of the economy in an attempt to mitigate the effects of the Great Depression during the administration of President
a. Theodore Roosevelt.
b. Franklin Roosevelt.
c. James Garfield.
d. Lyndon Johnson.

5) There are currently _____ Cabinet departments.
a. 10
b. 12
c. 13
d. 15

6) Who is responsible for establishing a department's general policy and overseeing its operations?
a. talking heads
b. Cabinet secretaries
c. agency advisors
d. policy wonks

7) The United States Postal Service is an example of a(n)
a. Cabinet department.
b. government corporation.
c. independent executive agency.
d. independent regulatory commission.

8) Rather than perform regulatory functions, independent executive agencies perform
a. oversight duties.
b. service.
c. revenue generating activities.
d. without congressional or presidential supervision or control.

9) The Securities and Exchange Commission (SEC) is an example of a(n)
a. independent executive agency.
b. government corporation.
c. clientele agency.
d. independent regulatory commission.

10) The relatively stable relationship and pattern of interaction that occurs among an agency, interest groups, and congressional committees is called a(n)

a.   issue network.
b.   implementation network.
c.   policy circle.
d.   iron triangle.

11)   Administrative discretion—the ability of bureaucrats to make choices concerning implementation of congressional intentions—is exercised through two formal administrative procedures:
a.   sunset review and administrative oversight.
b.   rule-making and issue networking.
c.   administrative adjudication and rule-making.
d.   congressional review and oversight.

12)   The bureaucracy has the ability to make choices about the best way to implement congressional or executive intentions, thus giving the bureaucracy tremendous leeway to carry out its assigned tasks. This ability is called
a.   administrative adjudication.
b.   administrative discretion.
c.   regulatory authority.
d.   legislative override.

13)   The president has the power to hold agencies accountable through
a.   appointments to the bureaucracy.
b.   reorganization of the bureaucracy.
c.   issuing executive orders.
d.   All of the above.

14)   Congress can hold the bureaucracy accountable through
a.   issuing executive orders.
b.   appointment and removal of bureau heads.
c.   investigation and appropriations.
d.   All of the above.

15)   All executive orders must be published in the
a.   *Wall Street Journal.*
b.   *New York Time.*
c.   *Federal Register.*
d.   *Federalist Papers.*

TRUE/FALSE

1)   The bureaucracy consists of a set of complex, hierarchical departments, agencies, commissions, and their staffs that exist to help the president carry out the laws of the country.

2) The "spoils system" allowed each political party to pack the bureaucracy with its supporters when it won political office.

3) The passage of the Sixteenth Amendment significantly impeded the growth of the federal bureaucracy.

4) Governments exist for the public good, not to make money and, therefore, cannot be run like a business.

5) That the federal workforce is composed primarily of young, inexperienced workers and that this trend is worsening has been of concern to many in governmental authority.

6) Bureaucrats make, as well as implement, policies.

7) Regulations promulgated by executive branch agencies have the force of law.

8) Presidential appointments make up the vast majority of all federal jobs.

9) The bureaucracy is accountable to no one except the president.

10) Congress's power to control the bureaucracy is severely limited because Congress lacks the power of the purse.

SHORT ANSWER AND ESSAY QUESTIONS

1) Detail and briefly discuss the history and development of the executive bureaucracy from the early days of the country through the administration of Presidents Franklin Roosevelt and Lyndon Johnson.

2) What was the spoils system, and how did it lead to civil service reforms? What were those reforms?

3) What are iron triangles and are they as significant as they once were?

4) Does the bureaucracy make policy? Discuss two ways that it does or does not.

5) Discuss three methods by which the bureaucracy can be held accountable.

6) Discuss the roots and development of the federal bureaucracy.

7) What is the formal organization of the bureaucracy, and what are the main functions of each agency, commission, or department? Give examples.

8) Discuss the nature of bureaucratic policy making.

9) Discuss the checks and balances the president, Congress, and the judiciary have on the bureaucracy. Which techniques are used most often, and which are most effective and why?

10) What problems plague bureaucratic politics, and what reforms have been aimed at addressing them? How effective have these reform efforts been?

COMPARE AND CONTRAST

patronage, spoils system, and merit system

Cabinet departments, government corporations, independent executive agencies, and independent regulatory commissions

iron triangles and issue networks

administrative discretion and administrative adjudication

executive versus congressional control of the bureaucracy

ANSWERS TO STUDY EXERCISES

multiple choice answers

1.	a	p. 273
2.	c	p. 275
3.	d	p. 275
4.	b	p. 275
5.	d	p. 284
6.	b	p. 288
7.	b	p. 288
8.	b	p. 288
9.	d	p. 289
10.	d	p. 290
11.	c	p. 292
12.	b	p. 292
13.	d	p. 294, 295
14.	c	p. 295
15.	c	p. 296

true/false answers

1.   T   p. 271
2.   T   p. 273
3.   F   p. 275
4.   T   p. 277
5.   F   p. 283
6.   T   p. 291, 292
7.   T   p. 292
8.   F   p. 294
9.   F   p. 295, 296
10. F   p. 295

CHAPTER 9
THE JUDICIARY

Chapter Goals and Learning Objectives

The role of the federal judiciary today, particularly the U.S. Supreme Court, differs dramatically from its function early in the nation's history. The "least dangerous branch" gained prominence from the development of the doctrine of judicial review and, as well, from the growth in the size and reach of the federal government. The Framers never envisioned the ambit and authority of the Supreme Court and lower federal courts; of course, the Framers never envisioned the incredible growth of the federal government and its laws, laws adjudicated by the federal courts. The Supreme Court today, as arbiter of the Constitution, can, in a single decision, dramatically reshape the social and political structure of the country as evidenced, for example, by *Roe* v. *Wade, Bush* v. *Gore* and *Lawrence* v. *Texas.* As our social and political beliefs change in the country, so does the interpretations of our laws by judges and justices on the federal bench. Who sits on the Supreme Court and in the federal courts across the nation truly matters. It is no wonder that many scholars believe the most lasting decision a president makes while in office is who he appoints to the Supreme Court and the federal bench.

This chapter is designed to give you an overview of the federal judicial system. The main topic headings in the chapter are:

- The Constitution and the Creation of the Federal Judiciary
- The American Legal System
- The Federal Court System
- How Federal Court Judges are Selected
- The Supreme Court Today
- Judicial Philosophy and Decision Making
- Judicial Policy-Making and Implementation

In each section, there are certain facts and ideas that you should strive to understand. Many are in boldface type and appear in both the narrative and in the glossary at the end of the book. Other ideas, dates, facts, events, people, etc. are more difficult to pull out of the narrative. (Keep in mind that studying for objective-style tests [multiple choice, T/F] is different than studying for essay tests. See the Study Guide section on test taking for hints on study skills.)

In general, after you finish reading and studying this chapter, you should understand the following:

- The Constitution and the creation of the federal judiciary—the Supreme Court by Article III and the lower federal courts by Congress starting with the Judiciary Act of 1789
- The American legal system and the civil and criminal law
- The federal court system, its types, and jurisdiction
- How federal court judges are selected by presidential nomination and Senate review and confirmation
- The operation and function of the Supreme Court today
- Judicial philosophy and decision making: how judicial decisions are reached based on legal and extra-legal factors
- How judicial policies are made and implemented

Chapter Outline and Key Points

In this section, you are provided with a basic outline of the chapter and key words/points you should know. Use this outline to develop a complete outline of the material. Write the definitions or further explanations for the terms. Use the space provided in this workbook or rewrite that material in your notebook. This will help you study and remember the material in preparation for your tests, assignments, and papers.

Hamilton, "the least dangerous branch"—

The Constitution and the Creation of the Federal Judiciary

Article III—

judicial review—

Marbury v. *Madison* (1803)—

Martin v. *Hunter's Lessee* (1816)—

jurisdiction of the U.S. Supreme Court—

Judicial Power of the Supreme Court (Table 9.1)—

Congress and the lower federal courts—

Chief Justice and impeachment—

life tenure with "good behavior"—

Federalists No. 78—

checks on the power of the judiciary—

The Judiciary Act of 1789 and the Creation of the Federal Judiciary

Judiciary Act of 1789—

litigants—

circuit court—

size of the Supreme Court—

John Jay—

first decade of the Supreme Court—

The Marshall Court: *Marbury* v. *Madison* (1803) and Judicial Review

John Marshall—

practice of issuing opinions—

Marbury v. *Madison* (1803)—

judicial review—

Marshall's argument for judicial review—

writ of *mandamus*—

The American Legal System

the judicial system of the United States—

trial courts—

appellate courts—

Jurisdiction

jurisdiction—

original jurisdiction—

appellate jurisdiction—

Criminal and Civil Law

      criminal law—

      government as plaintiff—

      civil law—

      plaintiff—

      defendant—

      what happens to most cases—

      judges during trial—

      juries—

<u>The Federal Court System</u>

      constitutional courts—

      legislative courts—

      Federal Court System (Figure 9.1)—

District Courts

      federal district courts—

      district court jurisdiction:

          1)

          2)

          3)

      U.S. attorney—

The Courts of Appeals

      U.S. Courts of Appeals—

      circuit courts of appeals—

118

eleven numbered courts of appeals—

D.C. Court of Appeals—

U.S. Court of Appeals for the Federal Circuit—

number of federal appellate judges in 2005—

jurisdiction of courts of appeals—

correct errors of law and procedure—

brief—

The Supreme Court

court of last resort—

role of Supreme Court—

decisions of Supreme Court binding on what?—

precedent—

stare decisis—

How Federal Court Judges are Selected

political process of selection—

How a President Affects the Federal Judiciary (Figure 9.3)—

senatorial courtesy—

Who are Federal Judges?

characteristics—

Appointments to the U.S. Supreme Court

constitutional requirements—

nominees encounter greater opposition than other federal judges—

Nomination Criteria

six criteria—

Competence—

    prior judicial experience (see Table 9.2)—

Ideological or Policy Preference—

    strict constructionist—

Pursuit of Political Support—

    Sandra Day O'Connor—

    Thurgood Marshall—

    Clarence Thomas—

    Jewish seat—

    Ruth Bader Ginsberg—

    Abe Fortas—

    religious background—

The Supreme Court Confirmation Process

power of the Senate—

simple majority vote for confirmation—

Investigation—

    FBI check—

Lobbying by Interest Groups—

    Robert Bork—

    involvement in lower federal court nominations—

The Senate Judiciary Hearings and Senate Vote—

committee recommendation to full Senate—

close votes in the full Senate—

The Supreme Court Today

public awareness of Court and members—

"cult of the robe"—

media coverage of the Court—

Deciding to Hear a Case   .

petitions received and opinions issued in 2003-2004 term—

How a Case Goes to the Supreme Court and What Happens After It Gets There (Figure 9.4)—

content and size of Court's docket from 1930s forward—

two types of jurisdiction of the Supreme Court—

substantial federal questions—

writ of *certiorari*—

Rule of Four—

two criteria petitions must meet for *certiorari*—

cert pool—

"discuss list"—

vote to accept a case—

The Role of Clerks—

what do clerks do? (Table 9.3)—

relationship between justices and clerks—

How Does a Case Survive the Process?

criteria for Court accepting a case—

amicus curiae—

The Federal Government—

solicitor general—

percentage of cases Court accepts where U.S. government is petitioner versus others—

Conflict Among the Circuits—

interest group participation—

Hearing and Deciding the Case

submission of legal briefs—

Oral Arguments—

when do oral arguments take place?—

who participates in oral arguments?—

how do justices use oral arguments?—

The Conference and the Vote—

traditions in the conference—

role of conferences—

majority vote wins—

Writing Opinions—

majority opinion—

who assigns task of writing majority opinion?—

importance of majority opinion—

plurality decisions—

concurring opinions—

dissenting opinion—

Judicial Philosophy and Decision Making

Judicial Philosophy, Original Intent, and Ideology

judicial restraint—

judicial activism—

Models of Judicial Decision Making

Behavioral Characteristics—

The Attitudinal Model—

The Strategic Model—

Public Opinion—

abortion cases—

Korematsu v. *U.S.* (1944)—

Youngstown Sheet & Tube Co. v. *Sawyer* (1952)—

U.S. v. *Nixon* (1974)—

public confidence in the Court—

Judicial Policy-Making and Implementation

Policy-Making

measures of the power of the Court—

political questions—

Implementing Court Decisions

judicial implementation—

implementation populations—

three requirements for effective implementation:

1)

2)

3)

Research Ideas and Possible Paper Topics
---

1)   Research the Court's current docket (see official Supreme Court Web site below). How many cases will it hear? What types of cases will the Court hear? What constitutional issues are at stake? Why do you think the Court has chosen to rule on these cases?

2)   Research biographies on the current Supreme Court justices. What are their backgrounds? Why were they chosen for the Court and by whom? How are they perceived by court-watchers? (In other words, what do the experts think of them?) Is there a definite majority on the Court for any single set of constitutional issues? The Warren Court was characterized as very activist, particularly regarding due process rights. Can the Rehnquist Court be characterized? If so, how?

3)   Choose two well-known Supreme Court cases. Research to determine interest group activity and attempts at public persuasion on the Court during the cases. Using those examples and the text, write a paper (or prepare a short talk) about the impact of public opinion and lobbying on the Supreme Court.

4)   Research and analyze President Bush's judicial appointments. What type of judicial policy does Mr. Bush seek in a nominee? How have his nominees reflected the president's political opinions? How well have President Bush's nominees faired in the process of Senatorial confirmation?

5)   Constitutional law is taught textually. The language and nuance of what the Court says in its opinions is very important. Choose five cases and read the actual opinions. What types of language does the Court tend to use? Are rulings broad or narrow? Are precedents overturned? How does the Court use precedent generally? What did you learn about the Court from reading opinions?

Web Sites

The official Web site of the **Supreme Court of the United States** offers transcripts of oral arguments before the Court, recent case decisions, a history of the Court, the Court's docket, and other information.

     www.supremecourtus.gov

Oyez-Oyez-Oyez is a comprehensive database of major constitutional cases featuring multimedia aspects such as audio of oral arguments.
> http://www.oyez.org/oyez/frontpage

The site of the **Supreme Court History Society** covers the basic history of the Court and has a gift catalog.
> www.supremecourthistory.org

Findlaw is a searchable database of S.C. decisions plus legal subjects, state courts, law schools, bar associations, and international law.
> www.findlaw.com

Rominger Legal Services provides U.S. Supreme Court links, including history, pending cases, rules, bios, etc.
> www.romingerlegal.com/supreme.htm

FLITE: Federal Legal Information Through Electronics offers a searchable database of Supreme Court decisions from 1937-1975.
> www.fedworld.gov/supcourt/index.htm

U.S. Supreme Court Plus has decisions from the current term as well as legal research, bios, basic Supreme Court information, and more. Also offers a free e-mail notification service of Supreme Court rulings.
> www.usscplus.com

The Legal Information Institute offers Supreme Court opinions under the auspices of Project Hermes, the court's electronic-dissemination project. This archive contains (or will soon contain) all opinions of the court issued since May of 1990.
> http://supct.law.cornell.edu/supct/

The **Federal Judiciary Homepage** offers a wide variety of information about the U.S. Federal Court system.
> www.uscourts.gov

Law.com offers the latest Supreme Court news on its "United States Supreme Court Monitor" Web site. (Free registration is required.)
> http://www.law.com/jsp/scm/news.jsp

The American Bar Association provides analysis of the issues, arguments, background and significance of every case slated for argument in the U.S. Supreme Court.
> http://www.abanet.org/publiced/preview/home.html

C-SPAN also offers information about oral arguments before the U.S. Supreme Court.
> http://www.c-span.org/courts/oralarguments.asp

MULTIPLE CHOICE QUESTIONS

1) Article III establishes
   a. the Supreme Court.
   b. inferior courts.
   c. ten-year terms for federal judges.
   d. All of the above.

2) The three-tiered structure of the federal court system was established by
   a. Article III.
   b. Article IV.
   c. the Judiciary Act of 1789.
   d. the Hamilton Act.

3) The size of the Supreme Court is
   a. alterable only by constitutional amendment.
   b. set by Congress.
   c. set by the Constitution.
   d. All of the above.

4) Judicial review comes from
   a. the Judiciary Act of 1789.
   b. Article III.
   c. *Chisholm* v. *Georgia.*
   d. *Marbury* v. *Madison.*

5) Before a federal or state court can hear a case, the court must have
   a. standing.
   b. jurisdiction.
   c. review powers.
   d. precedent.

6) Federal district courts are courts of original jurisdiction, meaning that they hear
   a. cases only involving federal questions.
   b. appellate cases or trials.
   c. appellate cases.
   d. only trials, no appeals.

7) The court that handles most cases involving federal regulatory agencies is the
   a. First Circuit Court of Appeals.
   b. District Court.
   c. D.C. Court of Appeals.
   d. U.S. Court of Appeals for the Federal Circuit.

8) The reliance on past decisions to formulate decisions in new cases is based on the doctrine of
   a. *stare decisis.*
   b. *per curiam.*
   c. *amicus curiae.*
   d. *seriatim.*

9) Which of the following is an important criterion for nomination to the U.S. Supreme Court?
   a. competence
   b. ideology
   c. political support
   d. All of the above.

10) The original jurisdiction of the Supreme Court
   a. involves disputes between states.
   b. includes cases affecting ambassadors, public ministers, or a state.
   c. includes territorial disputes among states.
   d. All of the above.

11) Nearly all Supreme Court cases arrive at the Court through
   a. *in forma pauperis* petitions.
   b. original jurisdiction cases.
   c. writ of *certiorari.*
   d. informal request for review by state courts.

12) For the Court to accept a case on a writ of *cert*, the case typically
   a. involves a substantial federal question.
   b. comes from a state court of last resort, a special three-judge federal district court, or the U.S. Court of Appeals.
   c. is approved by four justices of the Supreme Court for review.
   d. All of the above.

13) The person responsible for handling appeals on behalf of the U.S. government before the Supreme Court is the
   a. solicitor general.
   b. attorney general.
   c. procurator.
   d. U.S. prosecuting attorney.

14) When a justice disagrees with the ruling of a Court majority opinion, he/she may write a
   a. concurring opinion.
   b. dissenting opinion.
   c. *per curiam* opinion.
   d. plurality opinion.

15) The idea that judges should refrain from making policy is referred to as
     a.   democratic theory.
     b.   delegation.
     c.   judicial restraint.
     d.   judicial activism.

TRUE/FALSE QUESTIONS

1)   The federal court structure is established in Article III.

2)   The Supreme Court has nine justices as stipulated in the Constitution.

3)   John Marshall was the first Chief Justice of the United States.

4)   The opinion by John Marshall in *Marbury* v. *Madison* (1803) dramatically increased the power and importance of the Supreme Court.

5)   In courts of original jurisdiction, judges are interested only in questions of law.

6)   The appellate courts hear new testimony to determine errors of fact.

7)   The traditional Jewish seat on the Supreme Court was vacant after the 1969 retirement of Justice Abe Fortas until the appointment of Ruth Bader Ginsburg.

8)   Around two-thirds of those Americans sampled in 2002 count not name any members of the United States Supreme Court.

9)   The Chief Justice of the Supreme Court always assigns the writing of opinions.

10) The Supreme Court is in no way subject to public opinion in its decision making.

COMPARE AND CONTRAST

original and appellate jurisdiction

Supreme Court's exercise of jurisdiction in its early days versus today

criminal and civil law

federal and state court systems

constitutional and legislative courts

writ of *certiorari* and *in forma pauperis*

opinions: majority, concurring, plurality, dissenting

judicial restraint and judicial activism

SHORT ANSWER AND ESSAY QUESTIONS

1) Discuss the facts and ruling in *Marbury* v. *Madison* and the significance of the case to American jurisprudence. Does opposition to the doctrine of judicial review still exist today? Research this latter question.

2) What impact did John Marshall have on the Court and the nation?

3) Define and discuss the concepts of jurisdiction and precedent.

4) What are briefs, and how do they affect the Supreme Court?

5) What kinds of opinions do the Supreme Court issue, and what are their effects?

6) Explain the basics of the American judicial system. How was it created, and what are its structures and rules?

7) How are federal judges and Supreme Court justices selected? Discuss fully the legal and political issues involved.

8) Discuss the jurisdictions of the Supreme Court and how cases reach that body.

9) What is the process by which the Supreme Court decides a case? Be sure to start at the process of getting on the docket and going through to the opinion stage.

10) What "extra-legal" factors shape judicial decision making?

ANSWERS TO STUDY EXERCISES

multiple choice answers

1.	a	p. 300
2.	c	p. 302
3.	b	p. 304
4.	d	p. 305
5.	b	p. 306
6.	d	p. 309
7.	c	p. 310
8.	a	p. 311

9.	d	p. 315
10.	d	p. 320, 321
11.	c	p. 322
12.	d	p. 322
13.	a	p. 324
14.	b	p. 326
15.	c	p. 327

true/false answers

1.	F	p. 302
2.	F	p. 304
3.	F	p. 304
4.	T	p. 305
5.	F	p. 306, 307
6.	F	p. 310
7.	T	p. 318
8.	T	p. 319
9.	F	p. 326
10.	F	p. 330, 331

CHAPTER 10
PUBLIC OPINION AND THE NEWS MEDIA

Chapter Goals and Learning Objectives

What opinions do you have about politics and government? Are they the same as those of your parents, your friends, of people down the street? Public opinion polls reveal that Americans are a diverse lot, but nonetheless, agree on many issues. Politicians and others who want to sway public opinion depend on public opinion polls to inform them of what Americans believe and want from their government and elected officials. This is nothing new. Politicians back in the time of the Framers did not have sophisticated public opinion polls to tell them what the citizens believed or wanted, nor did they have national news media to tell them the results of those polls, but they sought to mold public sentiment nevertheless. Both politicians and the people they lead seek to know where opinion is at a given moment and how it is formed.

Politicians and governmental leaders seek to sway opinion and inform the people of the country about their activities, often in a light to best portray them, regardless of the truth. That's why the news media is so important in our democracy. An essential function of the press is not just to pass on what politicians want you to hear, but to analyze and report to the American people on what your elected representatives are doing in Washington. That is why the news business is the only private business protected directly by the U.S. Constitution. The First Amendment protects the freedom of the press to report on the activities of our government. The manner in which they do it and how effectively they do it is another matter entirely.

The news media—the aggregate of electronic and print journalism—has the potential to exert enormous influence over Americans. The news media is crucial in facilitating public awareness of and discourse on politics necessary for the maintenance of a free country. The First Amendment grants the media broad rights. But is there a corresponding responsibility? Do citizens get the information from the news media we need to make educated decisions about elections? Does the news media provide complete, objective, issue-based coverage of politicians and public policy, or does it focus on the trivial, entertaining, and sensational?

This chapter is designed to give you a better understanding of polling and the nature of public opinion and to help you better understand from whence your own opinions, and the opinions of others, have come. It also is designed to give you a basic understanding of the opportunities, challenges, and problems posed by the news media today as well as the effects of our (the citizenry's) unthinking consumption of the media's messages. The main topic headings of the chapter are:

- Efforts to Influence and Measure Public Opinion
- Political Socialization and Other Factors That Influence Opinion Formation

- Why We Form Political Opinions
- How Public Opinion Is Measured
- The News Media
- The U.S. Media Today
- The Media's Influence on the Public
- The Public's Perception of the Media
- Government Regulation of the Electronic Media

In each section, there are certain facts and ideas that you should strive to understand. Many are in boldface type and appear in both the narrative and in the glossary at the end of the book. Other ideas, dates, facts, events, people, etc. are more difficult to pull out of the narrative. (Keep in mind that studying for objective tests [multiple choice, T/F] is different than studying for essay tests. See the Study Guide section on test taking for hints on study skills.)

In general, after you finish reading and studying this chapter, you should understand the following:

- What public opinion is and what its role is in determining public perception of issues
- Efforts to influence and measure public opinion for the purpose of gauging and swaying public opinion for political purposes and how public opinion is measured
- How the media influences on the public and public opinion
- Government regulation of the electronic media

Chapter Outline and Key Points

In this section, you are provided with a basic outline of the chapter and key concepts and terms you should know. Use this outline to develop a complete study guide for the chapter. Use the space provided in this workbook to write notes from your reading, defining the terms and explaining the concepts listed below. You may wish to rewrite the material in your notebook or computer. However you work up this outline, the effort and information will help you study and remember the material in preparation for your tests, assignments, and papers.

Efforts to Influence and Measure Public Opinion

public opinion—

Woodrow Wilson and public opinion—

Committee on Public Information—

Early Efforts to Measure Public Opinion

    public opinion polls—

    Literary Digest—

    straw polls—

    three errors in straw polling by *Literary Digest*:

        1)

        2)

        3)

    George Gallup—

Recent Efforts to Measure Public Opinion

    1848 presidential race and problem with polling—

    "Dewey Defeats Truman" headline—

    Success of the Gallup Poll in Presidential Elections (Figure 10.1)—

    2000 election—

<u>Political Socialization and Other Factors That Influence Opinion Formation</u>

    political socialization—

    factors that influence political socialization—

The Family

    two factors linked to the influence of the family on political
    socialization—

    parental influence greatest from birth to age five—

    political socialization by age 11—

School and Peers

elementary school influence—

peers—

peer group increasingly important as child gets older (past age five)—

high school influence—

better-informed citizens vote more as adults—

college influence—

liberalizing influence of college due to what?—

ideological self-identification of first-year college students (Figure 10.2)—

The Mass Media

as socialization agent—

impact of TV—

impact of alternative sources of political information on TV—

role of Internet—

Social Groups

group effects—

Religion—

effects of organized religion in today's society—

Ideological Self-Identification of Protestants, Catholics, and Jews (Figure 10.3)—

"the silent majority"—

Race and Ethnicity—

Racial and Ethnic Attitudes on Selected Issues (chart, p. 347)—

Gender—

Gender Differences on Political Issues (Table 10.1)—

Age—

effect of graying of America—

older people vote more regularly—

Group-Identified Voting Patterns in the 2004 Presidential Election (Figure 10.4)—

Region—

immigration—

differences between South and North—

the West—

Impact of Events

November 22, 1963—

Nixon's resignation—

effects of 9/11/01—

Political Ideology and Public Opinion About Government

political ideology—

conservatives—

liberals—

Why We Form Political Opinions

Personal Beliefs

"I"-centered—

what effects attitudes on issues that do not affect someone individually—

issues that do not affect someone individually and do not involve moral issues—

Political Knowledge

reciprocal effect—

Americans' level of knowledge about history—

Walter Lippman—

V.O. Key—

Cues from Leaders

low levels of knowledge can lead to rapid opinion shifts on issues—

role political leaders play in influencing public opinion—

president and bully pulpit—

How Public Opinion Is Measured

public opinion polls—

Creating a Public Opinion Poll

Determining the Content and Phrasing of the Questions—

Selecting the Sample—

random sampling—

stratified sampling—

Contacting Respondents—

telephone polls—

random-digit dialing surveys—

individual, in-person interviews—

Political Polls

 Push Polls—

 Tracking Polls—

 Exit Polls—

Shortcomings of Polling

 Sampling Error—

  poor and homeless underrepresentation—

  margin of error—

  all polls contain errors—

 Limited Respondent Options—

 Lack of Information—

  filter question—

 Intensity—

The News Media

The Evolution of Journalism in the United States

 journalism—

 first newspapers in the United States—

 Federalists, Anti-Federalists, and the press—

 fourth branch of government—

 First Amendment and the press—

 early partisan press—

 Washington's condemnation of the press—

 Benjamin Day's *New York Sun*, the forerunner of modern newspapers—

the sensational and the scandalous—

William Randolph Hearst—

yellow journalism—

muckraking—

payoffs to the press—

role of corporate profit—

technological changes—

electronic media supplants newspapers and magazines—

The U.S. Media Today

print press—

electronic media—

Print Media

increase in number of journalists covering Washington—

decline of newspaper circulation and readership—

newspaper chains and decline in competition—

Distribution of News Source Usage by Individuals (Figure 10.6)—

role of cable television—

niche journalism—

C-SPAN—

local television news growth and lack of substance—

rise of Internet as source of news and information—

traditional news media on Internet—

U.S. government on Internet—

alternative media on Internet—

The News Generation Gap (Table 10.2)—

Al-Jazerra—

How the Media Cover Politicians and Government

How the Press and Public Figures Interact—

> press release—

> press briefing—

> press conference—

Covering the Presidency—

> first among equals branches in coverage—

> Franklin D. Roosevelt and the bully pulpit—

> negative coverage of presidency—

> Eisenhower's invitation to "nail him to the cross"—

> George W. Bush pride in limiting public access to his administration by drastically limiting press access—

Covering Congress—

> why it is difficult for news media to survey Congress—

> news media focuses on three groups in covering Congress—

> > 1)

> > 2)

> > 3)

> coverage of investigative committee hearings:

> McCarthy—

Abu Ghraib in 2004—

The Judiciary—

    cloaked in secrecy—

    Supreme Court—

    presidential nominations to the Supreme Court—

Investigative Journalism and the Character Issue

Watergate scandal—

public perception of the press after Watergate—

character issue—

character trend in report supported by certain assumptions held by
the press:

    1)

    2)

    3)

fear of libel—

New York Times v. *Sullivan* (1964)—

actual malice—

Are the Media Biased?

"media bias"—

claims of liberal bias—

characteristics of reporters—

bias coming from effects of increasing fragmentation and competition
in media—

ideological fragmentation of media—

ideological Web sites on the Internet—

blogs and bloggers—

deepest bias is desire to the a good story—

politicians change "bias" as a political ploy—

wealth and celebrity status of media and bias—

The Media's Influence on the Public

effect of media on the public—

what limits ability of news media to sway public opinion—

media effects—

how media-influenced changes might occur:

1)

2)

3)

The Public's Perception of the Media

low public confidence in news media—

perception of media as politically biased—

credibility ratings for national news media—

public values the watchdog role of media—

Top Problems Facing Journalism (Table 10.3)—

nonprofit organizations research on media—

Government Regulation of the Electronic Media

two reasons for unequal treatment of print and broadcast media—

1996 Telecommunications Act—

FCC—

2003 changes by FCC allowing media corporations to own more of different kinds of media in a given market—

Content Regulation

content regulation—

equal time rule—

2000 FCC rules and court decision on requiring broadcasts to give candidates change to respond to personal attacks and political endorsements by a station—

Prior Restraint

prior restraint—

Pentagon Papers—

New York Times v. *U.S.* (1971)—

Justice Hugo Black in concurring opinion—

Research Ideas and Possible Paper Topics

1)   Use the library or Internet to find a number of polls. Bring them to class and, in discussion groups, analyze the quality and reliability of those polls. Be sure to discuss sampling, error rates, question wording, how respondents are contacted and other factors that affect the results.

2)   Write a paper based on your own political ideology and opinions. How were they formed? Consider those who have influenced these opinions and political views. Is the text correct in asserting what the dominant factors of political socialization are? Compare your experiences with those of your classmates.

3)   As a class project, choose an issue of interest and formulate your own poll. Then, administer it on campus. Discuss the process, the results, and problems of your poll, and extrapolate that to polling in general.

4)   For several days, tape each of the major networks' newscasts (ABC, CBS, NBC) and the two largest non-networks (FOX and CNN). View at least two days of each broadcast. Pay attention to the order and length of each story, the tone of the

report, and the graphics/images used. How are these broadcasts similar or different? Which reports seem most objective and why? What kinds of information are they offering? Is it the type of information you need to make educated decisions about politics and world affairs? Why or why not?

5) Locate several blogs on the Internet that focus on news and current events. What types of information are you finding there? Does it differ from more traditional types of media? How and why?

6) Examine the history of corporate consolidations of broadcast news media outlets over the past several decades. Examine examples of what critics of the corporatization of news coverage claim are ways in which diminishing diversity in media coverage of the news hinders your ability to get different viewpoints on critical issues. Discuss how would this hinder the free exchange of ideas in a democracy and, thus, undermine personal freedoms.

Web Sites

The **Gallup Organization** is one of the best-known and most well-respected polling agencies. Their Web site offers access to reports, polling data, and more about a variety of issues.
www.gallup.com

The **National Election Study** at the University of Michigan offers regular polls on elections, voting behavior, and electoral issues.
www.umich.edu/~nes

The **National Opinion Research Center (NORC)**, a research arm of the University of Chicago, offers surveys of American attitudes and opinions.
www.norc.org

Roper Center for Public Opinion Research, located at the University of Connecticut, is the largest library of public opinion data in the world. The Center's mission focuses on data preservation and access, education, and research. Includes the GSS—General Social Survey.
www.ropercenter.uconn.edu

The **Subject Guide to Political Socialization and Political Culture** is a Web site hosted by Appalachian State University.
http://www.library.appstate.edu/reference/subjectguides/polsoc.html

The **Washington Post Data Directory** is a guide to public opinion data published on the Internet by nonpartisan organizations.
www.washingtonpost.com/wp-srv/politics/polls/datadir.htm

The **Research Industry Coalition** is an organization promoting professionalism and quality in public opinion and marketing research. Their Web site includes an interesting article on the problems with the proliferation of "call in" polls and 900 number polls.

www.researchindustry.org/index.html

The **American Association for Public Opinion Research** is a professional association that publishes *Public Opinion Quarterly* whose tables of contents are available on this Web site.

www.aapor.org

Fairness and Accuracy in Reporting (FAIR) is a liberal watchdog group looking for media bias. In their own words: "FAIR believes that independent, aggressive, and critical media are essential to an informed democracy. But mainstream media are increasingly cozy with the economic and political powers they should be reporting on critically. Mergers in the news industry have accelerated, further limiting the spectrum of viewpoints that have access to mass media. With U.S. media outlets overwhelmingly owned by for-profit conglomerates and supported by corporate advertisers, independent journalism is compromised." The Web site offers examples of bias and more.

www.fair.org

Media Research Center is a right-wing organization that claims the media have a liberal bias. Offers links to conservative media and political sites.

www.mediaresearch.org

Media Matters for America is a comprehensive Internet site that reports on corporate and conservative bias in the news media. It was started by former conservative journalist David Brock. Updated daily.

http://mediamatters.org/

The Pew Center for People and the Press is an independent opinion research group that studies attitudes toward the press, politics, and public policy issues. Its Web site offers the results of numerous surveys including those of public attitudes toward the media's coverage of politics and offers information trends in values and fundamental political and social attitudes.

www.people-press.org

The **Annenberg Public Policy Center** at the University of Pennsylvania conducts content analysis on TV coverage of politics.

http://www.annenbergpublicpolicycenter.org

The Center for Media Literacy encourages critical thinking about the news media including media values.

www.medialit.org

Freedom Forum is an organization that champions freedom of the press under the First Amendment. This Web site provides a significant amount of full-text information (journal articles, press releases, study reports) about press freedom issues.
www.freedomforum.org

Practice Tests

MULTIPLE CHOICE QUESTIONS

1) An unscientific survey used to gauge public opinion on issues and policies is called a
   a. deliberative poll.
   b. exit poll.
   c. straw poll.
   d. public opinion poll.

2) The popular magazine that from 1920 to 1932 correctly predicted the outcome over every presidential election based on unscientific surveys of public opinion was
   a. *The American Voter.*
   b. *The Voice of the People.*
   c. *Public Opinion and American Democracy.*
   d. *Literary Digest.*

3) The founder of modern-day polling who correctly predicted the 1936 election was
   a. Louis Harris.
   b. George Gallup.
   c. Steve Roper.
   d. Walter Lippman.

4) The influence of family on political socialization stems from
   a. communication.
   b. receptivity.
   c. time with parents.
   d. All of the above.

5) During middle and high school, the most important political influences on kids come from
   a. events.
   b. parents.
   c. peers.
   d. media.

6) Most first-year college students identify themselves as being
   a. liberal.

b.   conservative.

c.   far right.

d.   middle of the road.

7)   One reason politicians and the news media have regular opportunities to influence public opinion is because

      a.   of the deep trust Americans place in the integrity and reliability of political and media sources.

      b.   of the lack of deep conviction with which most Americans hold many of their political beliefs.

      c.   of the deep conviction with which most Americans hold many of their political beliefs.

      d.   All of the above.

8)   The Founders placed such importance in the value of a free exchange of ideas in a democratic society that, despite the written assaults many received from the press, the Founders guaranteed freedom of the press in

      a.   the Preamble to the Constitution.

      b.   Article I of the Constitution.

      c.   the First Amendment of the Constitution.

      d.   the Fifth Amendment of the Constitution.

9)   Studies indicate that _____ contains the least substantive coverage of current events.

      a.   local television news.

      b.   radio news.

      c.   cable news.

      d.   news magazines.

10)   The element of the federal government receiving the most coverage by the news media is the

      a.   Supreme Court.

      b.   Congress.

      c.   president.

      d.   bureaucracy.

11)   In which 1964-case did the Supreme Court rule that for public figures to claim libel there must not only be a defamatory falsehood but also actual malice, making it much harder for public figures to prove libel?

      a.   *New York Times* v. *United States*

      b.   *New York Times Co.* v. *Sullivan*

      c.   *United States* v. *Nixon*

      d.   *Near* v. *Minnesota*

12)   A disproportionate number of journalists are

      a.   Republicans

b.   Democrats
c.   independents
d.   neocons

13)   With regard to the news media's influence on the public, the news media can
   a.   sway people who are uncommitted and have no strong opinion initially.
   b.   have a greater impact on topics far removed from the lives and experience of viewers and readers.
   c.   help tell us what to think about, even if they cannot determine what we think.
   d.   All of the above.

14)   Which of the following is not true about the public's perception of the news media?
   a.   Americans continue to value the watchdog role that the news media serve.
   b.   The news media ranks far below the military and the president in the level of confidence the American people have for those institutions.
   c.   The public's perception of the news media is as much a function of their ideological stance as it is a response to media content.
   d.   A substantial majority of the public thinks that the news media's influence on politicians through press scrutiny is decreasing rather than increasing.

15)   Why are the electronic media regulated by the government and the print media are not?
   a.   The airwaves used by the electronic media are considered public property.
   b.   The airwaves used by the electronic media are leased by the federal government to private broadcasters.
   c.   The airwaves used by the electronic media used by the electronic media are in limited supply and without regulation frequency signals would interfere with one another.
   d.   All of the above.

TRUE/FALSE QUESTIONS

1)   Presidents as early as Woodrow Wilson recognized the power of public opinion and tried to control it.

2)   George Gallup correctly predicted the winner in the presidential election of 1936.

3)   The fastest-growing age group, and that most likely to vote, is citizens over 65.

4)   Region has no effect on voter attitudes and political opinions.

5)   Events can have a very strong effect on political attitudes and values.

6)   The accuracy of any poll depends on the quality of the sample that was drawn.

7)   The media have the potential to exert enormous influence over Americans.

8)   Muckraking is a form of newspaper publishing that featured pictures, comics, color, and sensationalized, oversimplified news coverage.

9)   The news media rarely covers Congress, which is why there are only a few dozen members of the congressional press corp.

10)   The government rarely can impose prior restraints on the press.

COMPARE AND CONTRAST

agents of political socialization: family, mass media, school and peers, events, social groups, and political ideology

random sampling and stratified sampling

telephone polls and in-person polls

tracking polls, exit polls, straw polls, and deliberative polls

sampling error and margin of error

yellow journalism and muckraking

the national news media and the local news media

print press and electronic media

networks, affiliates, and wire services

media coverage of the president, Congress, and judiciary

government regulation of the news media: print and electronic

SHORT ANSWER AND ESSAY QUESTIONS

1)   What is political ideology?

2)   Compare and contrast the various ways of sampling used in polls.

3) What is public opinion? How do we measure it, and how accurate are those measurements?

4) Discuss the various processes of political socialization. What factors affect our opinion formation, and how do these factors affect the broader political system?

5) How do we form political opinions and ideologies? What is the relationship between opinion and ideology?

6) How do we measure public opinion? Discuss methods of sampling, polling, and their shortcomings.

7) Discuss the impact of media mergers on the amount and types of information available to American citizens.

8) What kind of influence do the media have on the public's attitudes and opinions?

9) The media today consist of a number of types of media. What are they, and how do they differ? How are they similar? Under what incentives do they operate, and how do they decide what to use and what not to use?

10) Compare and contrast the ways in which the media cover the three branches of government.

ANSWERS TO STUDY EXERCISES

multiple choice answers

1.	c	p. 339
2.	d	p. 339
3.	b	p. 339
4.	d	p. 341
5.	c	p. 343
6.	d	p. 352
7.	b	p. 354
8.	c	p. 361
9.	a	p. 365
10.	c	p. 368
11.	b	p. 371
12.	b	p. 372, 373
13.	d	p. 376, 377
14.	d	p. 378
15.	d	p. 381

true/false answers

1. T p. 338
2. T p. 339
3. T p. 349
4. F p. 349
5. T p. 351
6. T p. 359
7. T p. 360
8. F p. 362
9. F p. 369
10. T p. 381

CHAPTER 11
POLITICAL PARTIES AND INTEREST GROUPS

Chapter Goals and Learning Objectives

It is difficult to ignore the assertion of some scholars that we are now entering a new, more fluid era of party politics. But, while some maintain that our two-party system is likely to be replaced by a chaotic multiparty system, or by a system in which presidential hopefuls bypass party nominations altogether and compete on their own, it is important to remember that political parties have been staples of American life since the late 1700s. Virtually all the members of the states' legislatures and the U.S. Congress are members of either the Democratic or Republican Party, and they make the laws that govern elections and have long been disposed to protecting the grip the two-party system has on elective government in the country. So, in one form or another, the dominance of the two-party system will continue.

We also seem to be in an era of increasing isolation and fragmentation. Fewer Americans are joining interest groups, yet more individuals are trying to pressure policy makers at all levels of government. And the influence of corporate interest groups on political decision making seems to be increasing. What are interest groups today, and what roles do they play? Do they supplement and complement political parties? Do they enhance representation? Or, are they vehicles for powerful and wealthy interests to take over policy making?

This chapter is designed to give you an overview of political parties and interest groups, as well as how they have changed over time. The main topic headings of the chapter are:

- The Evolution of American Party Democracy
- Political Parties
- Interest Groups
- The Roots and Development of American Interest Groups

In each section, there are certain facts and ideas that you should strive to understand. Many are in boldface type and appear in both the narrative and in the glossary at the end of the book. Other ideas, dates, facts, events, people, etc. are more difficult to pull out of the narrative. (Keep in mind that studying for objective tests [multiple choice, T/F] is different than studying for essay tests. See the Study Guide section on test taking for hints on study skills.)

In general, after you finish reading and studying this chapter, you should understand the following:

- The history and evolution of American political parties

- The roles of American parties in our political system
- The basic structure of the two major American political parties: the Republicans and Democrats
- The history and evolution of interest groups and what interest groups are
- Strategies and tactics used by interest groups to further their agenda and how much influence they actually have
- The factors that contribute to interest group success

Chapter Outline and Key Points

In this section, you are provided with a basic outline of the chapter and key words/points you should know. Use this outline to develop a complete outline of the material. Write the definitions or further explanations for the terms. Use the space provided in this workbook or rewrite that material in your notebook. This will help you study and remember the material in preparation for your tests, assignments, and papers.

James Madison, *Federalist No. 10*, and factions—

political party—

interest group—

The Evolution of American Party Democracy

George Washington's farewell warning—

Hamilton's Federalists—

Jefferson and Madison's Anti-Federalists—

Democrats and Andrew Jackson—

Whigs—

Republicans and Abraham Lincoln—

Democrats and Republicans: The Golden Age

central traits of the "Golden Age"—

machines—

social advancement via the parties—

greatest party-line voting ever achieved in Congress—

The Modern Era Versus the Golden Age: Is the Party Over?

government's gradual assumption of key functions of parties—

Franklin Roosevelt's New Deal—

direct primary—

civil service laws—

issue-oriented politics—

ticket-split—

television and decline of parties—

The Two-Party System and Third Parties

one-party elections—

third-partyism—

Dixicrats—

Green Party—

Bull Moose Party—

George Wallace—

2004 congressional elections—

minor-party candidates for a House seat most likely to emerge under three conditions:

1)

2)

3)

when do third parties do best?—

United States is the only major Western nation that does not have at least one significant, enduring national third party—

The Basic Structure of American Political Parties

Political Party Organization in America: From Base to Pinnacle (see Figure 11.2)—

National Committees)—

   national convention—

   Democratic National Committee (DNC)—

   Republican National Committee (RNC)—

   party platform—

   Senate and House party caucuses or conferences—

State and Local Parties—

   most governmental regulation of parties left to the states—

   most party leadership positions are at the state and local level—

   pyramid arrangement—

   precinct—

   state central (or executive) committee—

Party Identifiers and Voters—

   no universal party membership—

   party has no control over or accurate accounting of its adherents—

   party identification—

   partisan affiliation seen as a convenience rather than a necessity for most Americans—

   legal and other factors limiting choice between the two parties—

   importance of party identification—

Sources of Party Identification—

    Who Belongs to the Republican and Democratic Parties? (Table 11.1)—

    parents are greatest influence—

    effect of charismatic political figures—

    social class—

The Role of Political Parties in the United States

Mobilizing Support and Gathering Power—

    how parties aid office holders—

    coalition—

A Force for Stability and Moderation—

Unity, Linkage, and Accountability—

    parties help compensate for the fragmentation of the U.S. government as designed by the Framers of the Constitution—

    links all the institutions of power—

    candidates must account for their performance at party-sponsored forums, primaries and conventions—

The Electioneering Function—

    Republican organizational strengths—

    importance of fund-raising—

    fund-raising skills of the two parties—

    polling my national parties—

    in-house media operations—

Policy Formulation and Promotion—

national party platform—

Selected Contrasts in the 2004 Party Platforms (Table 11.2)—

Legislative Organization—
party most visible and vital in the U.S. Congress—

election of congressional leaders—

the two parties organize and operate the Congress—

leaders advance legislations to further party's interests—

party affiliation most effect indicator of a member's votes—

reasons for the recent growth of congressional party unity and cohesion—

Interest Groups

increase in big business and trade groups lobbying—

"bowling alone"—

social capital—

civic virtue—

purpose of interest groups—

Why and How Interest Groups Form and Maintain Themselves

"pressure group"—

organized interest—

disturbance theory—

"entrepreneurs"—

The Role of Leaders—

The Role of Patrons and Funding—

patron—

The Role of Members—

       organizations usually composed of three kinds of members—

       collective good—

       free rider problem—

The Roots and Development of American Interest Groups

       Women's Christian Temperance Union—

       Progressive movement—

       business groups organize to counter Progressive moves—

       organized labor—

       American Federation of Labor (AFL)—

       open shop laws—

       1914 Clayton Act—

       Congress of Industrial Organizations (CIO)—

       The Rise of the Interest Group State—

              public interest groups—

              ACLU—

              Common Cause—

              Public Citizen—

       Conservative Backlash: Religious and Ideological Groups—

              Moral Majority—

              Christian Coalition

              Office of Faith-Based and Community Initiatives—

              National Rifle Association—

What Do Interest Groups Do?

what interests groups do—

Lobbying—

Lobbying Congress—

Attempts to Reform Congressional Lobbying—

1947 Federal Regulation of Lobbying Act—

1995 Lobbying Disclosure Act—

how much spent to lobby Congress in 2004?—

Lobbying the Executive Branch—

importance of providing decision-makers with information—

link between interest groups and regulatory agencies—

capture of agencies by interest groups—

Lobbying in the Courts—

Grassroots Lobbying—

Protest Activities—

Election Activities

Candidate Recruitment and Endorsements—

EMILY's List—

Getting Out the Vote (GOTV)—

Rating the Candidate or Office Holders—

American Conservative Union—

Americans for Democratic Action—

Political Action Committees (PACs)—

Bipartisan Campaign Reform Act of 2002—

527 groups—

Research Ideas and Possible Paper Topics

1) As the textbook points out, the Republican Party has developed an extensive public relations and campaign training organization, as well as a highly efficient fund-raising effort. The Democratic Party has, particularly in the 2004 presidential election, exploited the Internet as a dynamic new communications and fund-raising tool. What are some of the other strengths and weaknesses in terms of organization, fund-raising, "get out the vote" operations and communications of the two major parties?

2) Go and visit, or invite to class, some local party activists. Ask them to talk to you about what they do in the party, why and how they got involved in politics, and the issues that they consider important. Does the information you learn jive with what you read in the text?

3) Find copies of the most recent national platforms for the two major parties. Compare them on a variety of issues. Then, look at public opinion polls to see how the party positions correspond to those of average Americans. What do you find? Why do you think that is the case?

4) Call, write, or visit the Web sites of a number of interest groups. What are they doing? What are their key issues and tactics? Who are their members? How many members do they have? How does this information correlate with what you have learned in this chapter?

5) Interview your member of Congress, or their staff members, about their views of interest groups and lobbyists (or have your professor invite them to class to discuss the issue). What do they say? How much access do lobbyists actually have? How much influence? What kinds of tactics work best with Congress?

6) Interview several lobbyists (or ask your professor to invite several lobbyists to talk to your class). Discuss how they see their job and what tactics work and which ones don't. What issues do they deal with, and what do they offer to politicians? How do they define a successful lobbyist? After talking with the professional lobbyists, what do you think about lobbying now? Does it seem less "unsavory"? Do the media do lobbyists justice in their coverage?

7) As a class project, form an interest group. Decide what issue(s) you will promote and how you will do so. What strategies and tactics would you use? How would you attract members? How would you ensure the success of your group?

Web Sites

The National Political Index features a Web page titled "Contacting Political Parties" with scores of links to the two major parties, third parties and minor parties, along with associated links.

> http://www.politicalindex.com/sect8.htm

University of Michigan Documents Center offers links to political parties; includes national and state parties, as well as links to congressional party leadership and platforms.

> http://www.lib.umich.edu/govdocs/polisci.html

Third Party Central offers links to third parties.

> www.3pc.net/index.html

Politics 1 offers links to political parties, campaign information, candidate information, and more. They also offer a free e-mail newsletter.

> www.politics1.com/parties.htm

Open Secrets, sponsored by the Center for Responsive Politics, maintains a searchable Washington lobbyist database.

> http://www.opensecrets.org/lobbyists/index.asp

Public Citizen, a nonprofit, nonpartisan consumer advocacy group, maintains a special interests reports page listed by industry group.

> http://www.citizen.org/congress/special_intr/index.cfm

The University of Michigan Document Center Web site on the 2004 elections offers a wide-ranging list of links on subjects relating to the election including campaign contributions and interest groups. Click, under the heading "Campaign," the "Lobby Groups," and "Lobby Group Ratings" links in particular.

> http://www.lib.umich.edu/govdocs/elec2004.html#activ

American Association of Retired Persons (AARP) is an interest and advocacy group devoted to the interests of those over 50.

> www.aarp.org

American Civil Liberties Union (ACLU) offers information on the entire Bill of Rights, including racial profiling, women's rights, privacy issues, prisons, drugs, etc. Includes links to other sites dealing with the same issues.

> www.aclu.org

AFL-CIO is the largest trade union organization in America. Their Web site offers policy statements, news, workplace issues, and labor strategies.

> www.aflcio.org

The United States **Chamber of Commerce** is a business-oriented interest group whose Web site offers articles of interest, policy information, and membership info.
www.uschamber.org

The **American Trial Lawyers Association** is an interest group for trial lawyers who support access for citizens to civil courts and which opposed business groups working to limit these rights. The Web site offers news and information for the reporters and citizens.
www.atla.org

Common Cause, founded by Ralph Nader, was one of the first public interest groups. They promote responsible government.
www.commoncause.org

Mexican American Legal Defense and Education Fund (MALDEF) Web site offers information on Census 2000, scholarships, job opportunities, legal programs, regional offices information, and more.
www.maldef.org

Native American Rights Fund (NARF) Web site offers profiles of issues, an archive, resources, a tribal directory, and treaty information, as well as a lot of other information.
www.narf.org

The **National Association for the Advancement of Colored People** (NAACP) Web site offers information about the organization, membership, and issues of interest to proponents of civil rights. Has sections on the Supreme Court, Census 2000, the Education Summit and includes links to other Web sites.
www.naacp.org

The **National Rifle Association (NRA)** is a highly effective interest group on behalf of its members. Its Web site offers information on gun ownership, gun laws, and coverage of legislation on associated issues.
www.nra.org

National Organization of Women (NOW) Web site offers information on the organization and its issues/activities including women in the military, economic equity, reproductive rights, and so on. They offer an e-mail action list and the ability to join NOW online. Also has links to related sites.
www.now.org

Public Interest Research Group (PIRG) is a public interest group that promotes issues such as the environment, anti-tobacco, and so on.
www.pirg.org

MULTIPLE CHOICE

1) The first American president elected as the nominee of a political party was
   a. John Adams.
   b. George Washington.
   c. Alexander Hamilton.
   d. Thomas Jefferson.

2) The country's first major national presidential nominating convention was held in 1832 by the
   a. Federalists Party.
   b. Whig Party.
   c. Democratic Party.
   d. Republican Party.

3) The power of political parties has been undercut by a variety of factors, including
   a. civil service laws.
   b. direct primaries.
   c. issue-oriented politics.
   d. All of the above.

4) Television, which has come to dominate politics in the United States, naturally emphasizes _____ rather than abstract concepts.
   a. economic issues.
   b. personalities.
   c. serious examination of the news.
   d. party labels.

5) Third parties often find their roots in
   a. economic protest.
   b. sectionalism.
   c. issues, ideology, and charismatic personalities.
   d. All of the above.

6) The segment of the United States government where the party is the most visible and vital is
   a. the presidency and the executive branch.
   b. the Congress.
   c. the federal courts.
   d. the bureaucracy.

7) In Congress, parties perform a number of functions, including
   a. enforcing absolute party discipline through the use of sanctions.

b.   providing leadership and organization. .
c.   decentralizing power in Congress.
d.   All of the above.

8)   The term used to describe the web of cooperative relationships among citizens, which facilitates resolution of collective action problems, is called
a.   civic virtue.
b.   social capital.
c.   association.
d.   interest group progress.

9)   Political scientist David Truman argues that interest groups form to counteract other groups that already exist. This theory is called
a.   patronage
b.   disturbance theory.
c.   potential group theory.
d.   group formation theory.

10)   Groups such as Common Cause are often categorized as
a.   public interest groups.
b.   single issue groups.
c.   economic issue groups.
d.   All of the above.

11)   During the 1960s and 1970s, interest groups often formed around issues important to groups such as
a.   organized labor and business groups.
b.   trade and professional associations.
c.   women and minorities.
d.   All of the above.

12)   Interest groups lobby the courts by
a.   giving money to Supreme Court reelection campaigns.
b.   hand-picking which Supreme Court justice will hear their case.
c.   selecting favorable gains from trade.
d.   filing *amicus curiae* briefs.

13)   According to data assembled by the Center for Responsive Politics, how much money was spent on lobbying for every member of Congress?
a. $500,000
b. $1 million
c. $2 million
d. $4 million

14)   A type of lobbying involving individual citizens who contact their representative directly in an effort to affect policy is known as

a.   grassroots lobbying.
b.   logrolling.
c.   pork barrel politics.
d.   franking.

15)   A federally registered group that raises funds to donate to the political process is known as a(n)
a.   political action committee.
b.   incommunicado group.
c.   Title IX organization.
d.   board of donors.

TRUE/FALSE

1)   James Madison in *Federalist No. 10* warned against the dangers of factions.

2)   President George Washington in his farewell address to the nation warned against the development of political parties.

3)   The United States is the only major Western nation that does not have at least one significant and enduring national third party.

4)   The Democratic and Republican Parties are structurally based in Washington and are primarily national organizations.

5)   Parents are the single greatest influence in establishing a person's first party identification.

6)   Party identification is rarely if ever affected by charismatic political figures.

7)   The Democratic and Republican Parties work together to create a unifying national policy platform.

8)   Congress is organized and operated essentially by party affiliation.

9)   Many effective lobbyists in Washington are former members of Congress, former staff aides, former White House officials, or former Cabinet officers.

10)   Interest groups are not permitted to lobby the courts.

COMPARE AND CONTRAST

the historical roots of the Democratic Party and the Republican Party

civil service laws, patronage, and spoils system

the role of parties in the presidency and in Congress

Republican strengths and Democratic strengths

Democratic platform and Republican platform

potential versus. actual group membership

collective goods and free riders

kinds of interest groups: economic, public, governmental
business groups, trade, and professional organizations

election activities of interest groups: endorsements, ratings, PACs

ESSAY AND SHORT ANSWER QUESTIONS

1) Discuss the political machines of the "golden age" of parties.

2) The heyday of the political party seems past. Discuss the factors that contributed to party decline.

3) What is the role of the national platform, and how is the platform treated by office holders, once elected?

4) What are the roles of political parties in the U.S. system?

5) What is a third party, and why do they tend to remain peripheral to the political system?

6) Discuss the basic structure of American political parties.

7) Compare and contrast the strengths and strategies of the Republican and Democratic parties.

8) Define interest groups, and discuss their functions.

9) Why do interest groups form? Discuss a number of theories and their rationales for group formation.

10) Compare and contrast potential vs. actual interest group membership.

ANSWERS TO STUDY EXERCISES

multiple choice answers

1. d   p. 386
2. c   p. 387
3. d   p. 390
4. b   p. 390
5. d   p. 391
6. b   p. 401
7. b   p. 401, 402
8. b   p. 403
9. b   p. 405
10. a   p. 410, 411
11. c   p. 411
12. d   p. 414
13. d   p. 415
14. a   p. 417
15. a   p. 418

true/false answers

1. T   p. 385
2. T   p. 386
3. T   p. 391
4. F   p. 393
5. T   p. 395
6. F   p. 397
7. F   p. 401
8. T   p. 402
9. T   p. 414
10. F   p. 415

CHAPTER 12
CAMPAIGNS, ELECTIONS, AND VOTING

Chapter Goals and Learning Objectives

Elections in America make the transfer of power peaceful and legitimate. The United States has more elections, more often, than any other country in the world. We also have the lowest turnout of the industrialized countries—fewer than half of our eligible voters vote on a regular basis. There are a wide variety of explanations for nonvoting. There are even those who claim that having a low voter turnout is a good thing and increases stability in the political system. Others argue that reform is necessary to increase voter turnout. This chapter will look at those arguments and others related to voting and elections.

American political campaigns are long and expensive. They also seem to turn a large number of voters off the process entirely. Some Americans perceive that a few wealthy donors and political action committees have disproportionate influence over the process. The art of electioneering seems to have become the science of polling and advertising. However, the goals of campaigning remain the same: getting individuals to vote for you. How candidates pursue this goal is also the subject of this chapter.

This chapter is designed to give you an overview of voting and elections in the United States. The main topic headings of the chapter are:

- Types of Elections
- Presidential Elections
- Congressional Elections
- Campaign Finance
- Voter Behavior
- Bringing It Together: The 2004 Presidential Campaign and Elections

In each section, there are certain facts and ideas that you should strive to understand. Many are in boldface type and appear in both the narrative and in the glossary at the end of the book. Other ideas, dates, facts, events, people, etc. are more difficult to pull out of the narrative. (Keep in mind that studying for objective-style tests [multiple choice, T/F] is different than studying for essay tests. See the Study Guide section on test taking for hints on study skills.)

In general, after you finish reading and studying this chapter, you should understand the following:

- The types of elections and patterns of voting
- Presidential and congressional elections, including primaries, conventions and delegates

- Campaign finance
- Voting behavior, with emphasis on patterns in voter turnout and vote choice

---

Chapter Outline and Key Points

In this section, you are provided with a basic outline of the chapter and key words/points you should know. Use this outline to develop a complete outline of the material. Write the definitions or further explanations for the terms. Use the space provided in this workbook or rewrite that material in your notebook. This will help you study and remember the material in preparation for your tests, assignments, and papers.

Types of Elections

primary elections—

closed primary—

open primary—

crossover voting—

raiding—

blanket primary—

runoff primary—

nonpartisan primary—

general election—

initiative—

referendum—

recall—

Presidential Elections

The Nomination Campaign

nomination campaign—

front-loading—

70 percent of all the delegates to both party conventions are now chosen by the end of this month during a presidential election year—

effects of front-loading on the nomination process—

"invisible primary"—

Selecting the Delegates—

>every four years—

>difference between primaries and caucuses—

>only a small proportion of delegates selected by state caucus—

>most states used presidential primaries—

Who Are the Delegates?—

>activists—

>they reflect the philosophy of their party—

>most Americans are moderates and pragmatists and, therefore, left underrepresented by party delegates—

The Party Conventions—

>held in summer of presidential election year—

>national TV coverage (less coverage than in years past; why?)—

>how conventions were different a few decades ago—

The General Election Campaign

>general election campaign—

>candidates seek support and funding—

>brief themes or slogans—

The Personal Campaign

    personal campaign—

    typical campaign day—

    strains of campaign life—

The Organizational Campaign

    organization campaign—

    campaign infrastructure—

    voter canvass—

    get out the vote (GOTV)—

    campaign manager—

    campaign consultants—

    finance chair—

    pollster—

    direct mailer—

    effect of candidate using professional campaign consultants—

The Media Campaign

    communications director—

    press secretary—

    media consultant—

    paid media—

    free media—

    positive ad—

    negative ad—

170

contrast ad—

spot ad—

growth of negative ads—

inoculation ads—

negative attitude of news media in campaigns—

news media obsession with "horse-race" aspects of campaign—

polls taken by news media—

Kennedy-Nixon, first TV debates—

The Electoral College: How Presidents Are Elected

Electoral College—

elector—

How the Electoral College Works (Table 12.2)—

Electoral College was result of compromise among the Framers of the Constitution—

three essentials reasons why the Framers constructed the Electoral College—

    1)

    2)

    3)

Early Problems with the Electoral College—

    fourth presidential election revealed flaw in Framers' Electoral College plan—

    Twelfth Amendment (1804)—

    Electoral College problems in 1824 election between John Quincy Adams and Andrew Jackson—

171

Electoral College problems in 1876 race between Rutherford B. Hayes and Samuel J. Tilden—

1888 race between Grover Cleveland and Benjamin Harrison—

Modern Problems with the Electoral College Today—

1976 election between Jimmy Carter and Gerald Ford—

2000 presidential election between Al Gore and George W. Bush—

three proposals for reforming the Electoral College following the controversial 2000 presidential election:

1)

2)

3)

Patterns of Presidential Elections

Party Realignments—

critical elections—

realignments accomplished in two main ways—

last confirmed major realignment—

Secular Realignment—

effect of decline of party affiliation—

dealignment period—

Congressional Elections

The Incumbency Advantage

incumbency—

congressional reelection rates—

2004 congressional elections and the power of incumbency—

foolhardy to challenge a House incumbent except under this circumstance—

Redistricting—

U.S. Census—

redistricting—

gerrymandering—

Supreme Court rulings on redistricting:

1)

2)

3)

Scandals, Coattails, and Midterm Elections—

effect of scandals—

decline of presidential coattail effect—

midterm election—

patterns of presidential year and midterm elections on Congress—

Campaign Finance

Federal Election Campaign Act (FECA)—

Bipartisan Campaign Reform Act of 2002 (BCRA)—

BCRA fast-track provision—

McConnell v. *FEC* (2003)—

Sources of Political Contributions

over $3.9 billion spent on presidential and congressional elections in 2004 alone—

Democrats versus Republicans in spending—

importance and difficulty of raising funds to run a modern campaign—

Average Campaign Funds Raised, Spent and Contributed in 2004
Congressional Races (Table 12.5)—

Individual Contributions—

> individual's maximum allowable contribution under federal law
> for congressional and presidential elections—

> individual's limitation on total in gifts to all candidates combined
> in calendar year—

> requirement on individuals who spend over $10 thousand to air
> "electioneering communications"—

Political Action Committee (PAC) Contributions—

> political action committees (PACs)—

> Expenditures by PACs in 2004 Election Cycle (Figure 12.3)—

> PACs hope to achieve what by their contributions?—

> PACs give primarily to incumbents; why?—

Political Party Contributions—

> to benefit candidates and to ensure party discipline in voting—

Member-to-Candidate Contributions—

> "leadership" PACs—

> limits on contributions—

Candidates' Personal Contributions—

> *Buckley* v. *Valeo* (1976)—

Public Funds—

> presidential campaigns—

matching funds—

limits—

Independent Expenditures—

hard money—

The Internet—

John McCain—

Internet and headaches for Federal Election Commission (FEC)—

Soft Money and Issue Advocacy Advertisements—

soft money—

banned by BCRA—

Future Campaign Finance Reform

527 political committees—

<u>**Voting Behavior**</u>

Patterns in Voter Turnout

turnout—

How America Votes (Table 12.6)—

Voter Turnout in Presidential and Midterm Elections (Figure 12.4)—

Education—

Income—

why wealthy people vote more regularly—

why lower-income people vote less often—

Age—

Twenty-Sixth Amendment—

low turnout by young people—

Race and Ethnicity—

African American voting patterns—

Hispanic voting patterns—

Caucasian voting patterns—

Interest in Politics—

Why is Voter Turnout So Low?

percentage of U.S. voter participation—

contributing factors for low voter participation rates:

too busy—

difficulty of registration—

difficulty of absentee voting—

number of elections—

Patterns in Vote Choice

Party Identification—

Candidate Evaluations—

Issue Voting—

Bringing It Together: The 2004 Presidential Campaign and Elections

extremely divided the nation—

The Party Nomination Battle

John McCain—

Al Gore—

Hillary Clinton—

Joseph Lieberman—

Richard Gephardt—

Bob Graham—

John Kerry—

John Edwards—

Carol Moseley Braun—

Howard Dean—

Dennis Kucinich—

Al Sharpton—

Wesley Clark—

key states of Iowa and New Hampshire—

impact of third parties—

The Democratic Convention

Kerry-Edwards—

Kerry's speech—

no significant post-convention bounce—

The Republican Convention

George W. Bush

Dick Cheney—

more moderates appear during convention—

Bush's speech—

modest post-convention bounce—

The Presidential Debates

first debate—

John Edwards, Dick Cheney debate—

second debate—

third and final debate—

The Fall Campaign and General Election

deadlocked—

key battleground states—

Bush attacks on Kerry—

Kerry attacks on Bush—

Election Results

TV coverage—

Ohio vote—

provision ballots—

Kerry's formal concession—

Turnout in the 2004 Election

highest rate since 1968—

major partisan divide seen as primary cause for high numbers—

despite efforts to turn out youth vote, only slight increase—

third-party effect almost nonexistent—

The Next Four Years

Bush wins with 51 percent of vote—

increases in Republican majority in House and Senate—

how Democrats rebuild—

Research Ideas and Possible Paper Topics

1) Many reform proposals argue that the U.S. should adopt proportional representation. In this method of election, voters choose a party list as opposed to an individual candidate. This method strengthens parties and tends to increase voter turnout and the number of parties in the political system. Among those countries that use PR are: Holland, Poland, and others. Research the nature of PR and how it might work, or why it would not work, in the United States.

2) Accusations of voter irregularities in Ohio and Florida surfaced soon after the November 2004 presidential election, some of which were tied to the new electronic voting technologies that critics claimed lacked sufficient verification procedures for recount and accuracy. What were some of the allegations of fraud in Ohio and with regard to electronic voting? What measures, if any, do you think should be taken to secure the integrity of electronic voting procedures? What measures should be taken to assure voters that their votes count in an election?

3) Many scholars argue that low voter turnout is due to electoral rules, frequency of elections, apathy, etc. Discuss how you would change these impediments to voting and discuss the impact increased voter turnout would have on the electoral process.

4) Look at several sources discussing the Electoral College. What reforms have been proposed? How useful is the Electoral College now? Would you advocate a different approach? Does it matter that a presidential candidate can lose the popular vote and still become president as in the 2000 election? Hold a debate in class on the merits of the various routes to reform.

5) The recall of Governor Grey Davis of California in 2003 and the subsequent election of Arnold Schwarzenegger as the new governor was an unprecedented example of the use of voter recall in recent times. What is a recall election? What precipitated this recall in California, and what were the partisan factors involved? Was this a harbinger for the future of elections or a unique event politically? What impact has this had on electoral politics?

Web Sites

Audit the Vote is a Web site which argues that the election system is deeply flawed. The Web site reports news about the right to vote, voting accuracy, and reform.
http://www.auditthevote.org/index.jsp

BlackBoxVoting.Org is a nonpartisan, nonprofit, 501c(3) organization which states that it is "the official consumer protection group for elections, funded by citizen donations." It focuses on information about irregularities in electronic voting technology.
http://www.blackboxvoting.org

Project Vote-Smart is a nonpartisan information service funded by members and nonpartisan foundations. It offers "a wealth of facts on your political leaders, including biographies and addresses, issue positions, voting records, campaign finances, evaluations by special interests." It also offers "CongressTrack," a way for citizens to track the status of legislation, members and committees, sponsors, voting records, clear descriptions, full text, and weekly floor schedules, as well as access to information on elections, federal and state governments, the issues, and politics. Includes thousands of links to the most important sites on the Internet.
www.vote-smart.org

The **National Election Studies** are a key source of data on voting behavior.
www.umich.edu/~nes

Campaigns and Elections magazine's Web site is oriented toward campaign professionals but is also useful to teachers and students. It offers articles, their table of contents from the print version, job opportunities, and more.
www.campaignline.com

The **Federal Election Commission (FEC)** Web site offers campaign finance information, a citizens' guide to political contributions, news and information about elections and voting. Includes data about state regulations on voting (registration and residency rules, etc.) as well as elections data from a variety of elections.
www.fec.gov

Rock-the-Vote is an organization dedicated to getting young people involved in politics.
www.rockthevote.org

The **League of Women Voters** provides information to voters across the country on state, federal, and local elections and works to encourage election reform and campaign finance reform. Their Web site offers an interactive section on election information.
www.lwv.org

The **Office of the Federal Register** coordinates the functions of the Electoral College on behalf of the Archivist of the United States, the States, the Congress and the American

people. This site assembles a variety of information and statistics on the Electoral College, past and present.
http://www.archives.gov/federal_register/electoral_college/index.html

The **Census Bureau** has information on voter registration and turnout statistics.
www.census.gov/population/www/socdemo/voting.html .

Practice Tests

MULTIPLE CHOICE

1) An primary election that is held to choose party's candidate and that allows only registered party members to vote is called a
   a. primary.
   b. closed primary.
   c. blanket primary.
   d. open primary.

2) In campaigns for the U.S. House of Representatives, the use of professional campaign consultants has been shown to have
   a. a positive impact on a candidate's fund-raising and final vote tallies.
   b. a negligible impact on a candidate's fund-raising and final vote tallies.
   c. significantly added to the overall cost of the campaign while having a negative effect overall on fund-raising and the outcome of the election.
   d. long-term repercussions making future reelection doubtful.

3) The Framers' of the Constitution designed the Electoral College to
   a. produce a nonpartisan president.
   b. cover both the nominating and electing phases of presidential selection.
   c. work without political parties.
   d. All of the above.

4) The Electoral College encountered significant problems in the election of 1800. What was done to remedy the problem of selecting a president of one party and a vice president of another?
   a. Congress passed the Presidential Selection Act of 1804.
   b. The Supreme Court ruled that the Electoral College was, in its original state, unconstitutional, and devised a new plan to remedy the problem.
   c. The Eleventh Amendment was proposed and ratified.
   d. The Twelfth Amendment was proposed and ratified.

5) As the Electoral College currently exists, if there is no majority in the Electoral College for a candidate, the election is decided by the
   a. popular vote.
   b. House of Representatives.

c.   Senate.

d.   Congress as a whole.

6)   Reelection rates for sitting House members is typically

a.   approximately 25%

b.   approximately 50%

c.   approximately 75%

d.   more than 90%

7)   If an incumbent member of Congress loses a reelection bid, the cause is most likely

a.   redistricting.

b.   logrolling.

c.   nautical wheeling.

d.   changing channels.

8)   In 1976, the Supreme Court ruled that no limit could be placed on a candidate's personal spending in an election campaign, due to free speech guarantees, in the case of

a.   *U.S.* v. *Nixon.*

b.   *Rockefeller* v. *U.S.*

c.   *Buckley* v. *Valeo.*

d.   *McConnell* v. *FEC.*

9)   Approximately what percent of eligible adults in the United States vote regularly?

a.   85

b.   70

c.   40

d.   15

10) Who of the following is most likely to vote in an election?

a   a lower-income American

b.   a wealthy American

c.   an American age 18 to 24

d.   an American with little education

11) In 1971, the voting age was lowered to eighteen nationally by

a.   the Nineteenth Amendment.

b.   the Twenty-Second Amendment.

c.   the Twenty-Sixth Amendment.

d.   an act of Congress.

12) Voter turnout in this country is low due to the

a.   difficulty of registration.

b.   difficulty of absentee voting.

c.   frequency of elections.

    d.   All of the above.

13)   From 1960 to 2000, the percent of the eligible electorate that voted in the presidential election
    a.   shrank from 62 percent to 51 percent.
    b.   increased from 51 percent to 62 percent.
    c.   remained about the same.
    d.   increased by 21 percent.

14)   American elections are increasing portrayed in the news media as
    a.   horse races with a focus on the candidate and not necessarily on the party.
    b.   debates over ideas and positions.
    c.   ideological struggles between the two parties.
    d.   meaningless to the operation of the national government.

15)   George W. Bush, who claims his 2004 reelection was a mandate, won the election
    a.   with 57 percent of the national vote.
    b.   with 51 percent of the national vote.
    c.   by winning the Electoral College vote but losing the national vote.
    d.   despite the resignation and indictment of his vice president just prior to the election.

TRUE/FALSE

1)   The United States probably conducts more elections for more offices more frequently than any other nation on earth.

2)   If no candidate in the initial primary wins a majority of the votes, many states will have a runoff election afterward between the two candidates who received the most votes.

3)   Front-loading of the primary schedule generally benefits the front-runners.

4)   Delegates to the two national party conventions strongly mirror the ideological intensity and socioeconomic characteristics of the majority of Americans.

5)   In all but two states, the presidential candidate who receives the most votes in the state on general election day wins all of that state's Electoral College votes.

6)   The last confirmed major political party realignment began with the end of the administration of Herbert Hoover and the start of the administration of Franklin Roosevelt.

7)   In midterm (or "off-year") elections, members of the president's party tend to gain a significant number of congressional seats.

8)   Soft money contributions, which have been banned by campaign finance reform law, have been replaced by the new 527 political committees as a means for wealthy donors to bypass limits on contributions.

9)   Less than half of eligible citizens ages 18 to 24 are even registered to vote.

10)   The United States has one of the lowest voter participation rates of any nation in the industrialized world.

COMPARE AND CONTRAST

primary and general elections

primaries versus caucuses

presidential and congressional elections

Democratic convention delegates and Republican convention delegates

Democratic and Republican platforms

party realignment and critical election

incumbency advantage, redistricting, scandals, and coattails

presidential year and off-year, midterm elections

participation: turnout, income, age, gender, race, interest

ticket-splitting and straight-ticket voting

campaign finance: individual vs. member vs. party vs. PAC contributions

public funds, matching funds, personal funds, voluntary contributions

ESSAY AND SHORT ANSWER QUESTIONS

1)   Explain the various types of primary elections. How are they similar and different, and why would a state choose one variant over another?

2)   What impact could regional primaries and front loading have on the process of nominating a president?

3)   What is the electoral college? Why is it often the subject of reform proposals?

4)   What is an incumbency advantage, and what events serve to lessen it?

5)   Compare and contrast the nature of primary and general elections, for both congressional and presidential candidates.

6)   Discuss the changing nature of the party conventions and how the Republican and Democratic conventions are similar and different.

7)   Discuss the role of party, in presidential elections, and the nature of party alignments.

8)   Discuss voting behavior and voter turnout. Who votes and why? What voting patterns exist? Why is voter turnout so low? Does low turnout matter?

9)   What are independent expenditures? What are the constitutional issues and concerns surrounding them?

10)   Discuss candidate debates. How effective are they? Are they truly debates? How might they be changed to make them more effective and useful?

ANSWERS TO STUDY EXERCISES

multiple choice answers

1.	b	p. 426
2.	a	p. 435
3.	d	p. 438
4.	d	p. 440
5.	b	p. 440
6.	d	p. 444
7.	d	p. 445, 447
8.	c	p. 452
9.	c	p. 455
10.	b	p. 455, 458
11.	c	p. 457
12.	d	p. 461
13.	a	p. 460
14.	a	p. 462
15.	b	p. 472

true/false answers

1.	T	p. 424
2.	T	p. 428
3.	T	p. 430
4.	F	p. 430, 431
5.	T	p. 438
6.	T	p. 443
7.	F	p. 447
8.	T	p. 454
9.	T	p. 458
10.	T	p. 460

CHAPTER 13
SOCIAL AND ECONOMIC POLICY

Chapter Goals and Learning Objectives

An essential role of government is to set and implement public policy, the course of action that the government takes in dealing with matters of public concern. We will examine the problems of recognition, agenda setting, policy formulation, adoption, and implementation, and the eventual translation of concern into law and public action. It also concerns the development of social welfare and economic policy in the United States, particularly in the last 100 years. Social welfare policies and programs are designed to provide people with protection against want and deprivation, to enhance their health and physical well-being, to provide educational and employment opportunities, and otherwise to enable them to lead more satisfactory, productive, and meaningful lives. These social policies are meant to benefit all members of society, but especially the less fortunate. The idea behind these policies is that these services are so worthy to society as a whole that they should be provided by the government regardless of the ability of the recipients to pay. The question of where the line should be drawn between government and individual responsibility for these services and goods is the essence and scope of social welfare policy development. With regard to economic policy, the government defines and protects property rights, provides a common monetary system, grants corporate charters, issues patents and copyrights, handles bankruptcies, maintains law and order, and protects the environment, as well as many other economic tasks.

This chapter is designed to give you a basic understanding of policy questions and policy formulation, social welfare policies, and economic policy in the United States. The main topic headings are:

- The Policy-Making Process
- Social Welfare Policy
- Economic Policy
- Stabilizing the Economy

In each section, there are certain facts and ideas that you should strive to understand. Many are in boldface type and appear in both the narrative and in the glossary at the end of the book. Other ideas, dates, facts, events, people, etc. are more difficult to pull out of the narrative. (Keep in mind that studying for objective-style tests [multiple choice, T/F] is different than studying for essay tests. See the Study Guide section on test taking for hints on study skills.)

In general, after you finish reading and studying this portfolio, you should understand the following:

- The elements of the policy process

- The importance of the various stages to policy-making and the creation of government policy
- Social welfare policy and government's involvement in the economy
- The government's role in stabilizing the economy

Chapter Outline and Key Points

In this section, you are provided with a basic outline of the chapter and key words/points you should know. Use this outline to develop a complete outline of the material. Write the definitions or further explanations for the terms. Use the space provided in this workbook or rewrite that material in your notebook. This will help you study and remember the material in preparation for your tests, assignments, and papers.

public policy—

The Policy-Making Process

Stages of the Policy Process

the policy process has seven stages:

1) problem—

2) agenda—

3) formulation—

4) policy adoption—

5) budgeting—

6) policy implementation—

7) policy evaluation

Stages of the Policy-Making Process (Figure 13.1)

Problem Recognition and Definition

a necessary criterion—

effects of perceptions on government—

definitions of the problem—

public policies seen as problems or causes of other problems—

Agenda Setting

agenda—

systemic agenda—

governmental or institutional agenda—

how problems move onto the governmental (institutional) agenda—

Policy Formulation

policy formulation—

routine formulation—

analogous formulation—

creative formulation—

Policy Adoption

policy adoption—

what's needed to achieve policy adoption—

policy adoption through means other than majority coalitions—

unilateral presidential decision-making—

presidential veto threat—

Budgeting

budgetary process—

effect of refusal to fund or inadequate funding—

policy and program review—

Policy Implementation

policy implementation—

authorized techniques by administrative agencies to implement public policies within their jurisdictions:

authoritative techniques—

incentive techniques—

capacity techniques—

hortatory techniques—

Policy Evaluation

policy evaluation—

judgments by policy makers—

more systematic, objective form of policy evaluation—

possible players in policy evaluation—

role of evaluation research and studies—

Social Welfare Policy

social welfare policy—

The Roots of Social Welfare Policy

product of twentieth century—

Great Depression of 1930s—

Income Security

Social Security Act of 1935—

three major component of 1935 Social Security Act:

1)

2)

3)

how old-age insurance program funded—

unemployment assistance and how this component of Social Security Act served two basic purposes—

two perceived flaws of the national system—

national health insurance proposed with Social Security Act of 1935—

Health Care

how governments in the U.S. had been active in health care—

National Marine Service (established in 1789)—

Medicare and Medicaid—

Social Welfare Policy

income security programs—

nonmeans-based program—

means-tested program—

how nonmeans-based programs work—

old age, survivors, and disability insurance—

Social Security tax—

unearned income—

Trustees of the Social Security Trust Fund 2002 report—

G.W. Bush and privatization

G.W. Bush's "Commission to Strengthen Social Security"—

three options provided by the "Commission to Strengthen Social Security":

1)

2)

3)

unemployment insurance—

how Social Security unemployment insurance works—

social insurance: means-tested programs—

supplemental security income (SSI)—

Personal Responsibility and Work Opportunity Reconciliation Act of 1996—

key provisions of the Personal Responsibility and Work Opportunity Reconciliation Act of 1996:

    1)

    2)

    3)

    4)

    5)

    6)

    7)

food stamp program—

purpose of initial food stamp program—

what average participant in food stamp program receives—

who qualifies for food stamps?—

The Effectiveness of Income Security Programs

entitlement programs—

types of programs—

what they have achieved—

characteristic of all democratic industrial societies—

Health Care

heath care for veterans and Indians—

National Institution of Health—

what U.S. government spent per person on health in 2002—

U.S. ranking in quality of health care across the world—

Medicare—

      Medicare Part A—

      Medicare Part B—

      prescription drug program—

Medicaid—

      what Medicaid covers that Medicare doesn't—

      how Medicaid funded—

      medically indigent—

The Cost of Health Care—

federal outlay on health care in 2003—

factors that contribute to the high and rising costs of health care:

      1)

      2)

      3)

      4)

      5)

Economic Policy
The Roots of Economic Policy

mixed free-enterprise economic system—

state regulation and promotion of economy—

economic growth after the Civil War—

Interstate Commerce Act of 1887—

trusts—

Sherman Antitrust Act of 1890—

The Progressive Era

Progressive movement—

Pure Food and Drug Act—

Meat Inspection Act—

Upton Sinclair's *The Jungle*—

laissez-faire

interventionist state—

New Deal and national government regulations—

Financial Reforms—

Glass-Steagall Act of 1933—

Banking Act of 1935—

FDIC—

Federal Reserve Board—

Securities Act of 1933—

Securities Exchange Act of 1934—

SEC—

Agriculture and Labor—

price supports—

Wagner Act—

NLRB—

Fair Labor Standards Act of 1938—

Industry Regulations—

Federal Communications Commission—

Civil Aeronautics Board—

Motor Carrier Act of 1935—

Economic and Social Regulations

economic regulation—

social regulation—

Consumer Product Safety Commission—

Congress based legislation on its commerce clause authority—

Deregulation

deregulation—

what deregulation, in theory, would do—

perceived defects in economic regulatory programs in 1950s and 60s—

Gerald Ford and deregulation—

expansion under Carter of deregulation—

Airline Deregulation Act of 1978—

savings and loan deregulation—

failure of Reagan administration—

cost to taxpayers of bailout of savings and loan industry—

corporate scandals—

George W. Bush refusal to set more controls on business—

Stabilizing the Economy

economic stability—

inflation—

recession—

monetary policy—

fiscal policy—

Monetary Policy: Regulating Money Supply

how government conducts monetary policy—

money—

Federal Reserve Board—

Federal Reserve System

Federal Open Market Committee—

Federal Reserve Banks—

Alan Greenspan—

reserve requirements—

discount rate—

open market operations—

"moral suasion"—

the president and the FRB—

Fiscal Policy: Taxing and Spending

fiscal policy—

total (aggregate) spending—

John Maynard Keynes—

discretionary fiscal policy—

Research Ideas and Possible Paper Topics

1) Go to the Web site of the House of Representatives or call your local representative's office. Find out what social welfare laws are on the agenda for this session of Congress. Choose one and follow it over the course of the semester. Pay attention to partisan issues, which interest groups get involved and how, which members of Congress sponsor the bill, and how this bill fits the policy process you have learned about in this chapter.

2) In the last five years, many of the responsibilities for social welfare policies have been delegated to the states. Choose three states and find out what they are doing regarding social welfare. Are the states different or similar in their approaches? Why?

3) Do some research on President Bush's plan to privatize Social Security. Based on what you have learned about the policy process, discuss what was successful and unsuccessful about his plan. What tactics and strategies did he use to promote this policy? How effective were they? What tactics and strategies have been used by the opponents of privatization to what success?

4) The United States has a mixed free enterprise system. How many other countries of the world have similar economies? Are they as successful as that of the United States? Do some research to determine the answers to these questions. What other types of systems exist? Are any of them "successful"? Why or why not?

5) The Chairman of the Federal Reserve Bank is often described as the most powerful man in America. Do some research to determine why he is so powerful, who he is, and what his policies are. Compare our Fed to the Central Bank of another country. Do they have similar powers?

Web Sites

The Social Security Administration (SSA) Web site has information rules, regulations, and policies of the federal government on social security, both active and proposed. It offers information for citizens, scholars, and recipients. The Web site also offers historical perspectives on social security and its funding.
> www.ssa.gov

The Social Security Network was a project started in 1997 as a resource for information and research on the Social Security program and the debate about its future by **The Century Foundation**. Its panel of researchers and scholar publish original research and other information about Social Security on its Web site.
> http://www.socsec.org

The **Concord Coalition** is a nonpartisan, grassroots organization dedicated to eliminating federal budget deficits and ensuring Social Security, Medicare, and Medicaid are secure for all generations; founded by Senators Paul Tsongas (D) and Warren Rudman (R). The Coalition Web site offers information about the debt and deficit, as well as some social policy issues. It also offers e-mail newsletters, grassroots initiatives, statistics, and more.
> http://www.concordcoalition.org

Northwestern University hosts a Web site about its **Poverty, Race and Inequality Program,** which features information about social welfare programs and policy.
> http://www.northwestern.edu/ipr/research/socialwelfare.html

The **Institution for Research on Poverty** of the University of Wisconsin studies social inequity and poverty. The IRP develops and tests social policy alternatives. Reports are available on this Web site.
> www.ssc.wisc.edu/irp

Federal Reserve Board Web site has basic information about the FRB, its structure, and purpose. Also has publications, announcements, lists of related Web sites, biographies of members, reports, and statistics.
> www.federalreserve.gov

Office of Management and Budget (OMB) Web site offers budget information, reports, testimony, regulatory policies, and more from the perspective of the administration.
> www.whitehouse.gov/OMB

Congressional Budget Office (CBO) Web site offers Congress' opinions on budget matters including statistics, reports, budget reviews, testimony, and more.
> www.cbo.gov

The **Council of Economic Advisors** Web site offers the Economic Report of the President and CEA publications, as well as basic information about the CEA and its members.

www.whitehouse.gov/cea

GPO Access offers the full text of many Government Printing Office publications on the Web, including the economic indicators prepared for the Joint Economic Committee by the Council of Economic Advisors; updated monthly. Among the growing list of titles available are the Federal Register, the Congressional Record, Congressional Bills, United States Code, Economic Indicators and GAO Reports.

http://www.gpoaccess.gov/index.html

The **Concord Coalition** is a nonpartisan, grassroots organization dedicated to eliminating federal budget deficits and ensuring Social Security, Medicare, and Medicaid are secure for all generations; founded by Paul Tsongas (D) and Warren Rudman (R). The Coalition Web site offers lots of information about the debt and deficit, as well as some social policy issues. They offer e-mail newsletters, grassroots initiatives, statistics, and more.

www.concordcoalition.org

The **Economic Policy Institute (EPI)** is a nonpartisan think tank devoted to economic issues. This Web site offers a variety of reports on economic issues and a monthly newsletter delivered by e-mail. Despite their self-classification as nonpartisan, their board of directors is predominantly left-leaning (liberal).

www.epinet.org

Practice Tests

MULTIPLE CHOICE QUESTIONS

1) Political struggle often occurs at this stage of the policy process because how a problem is defined helps determine what kind of action is appropriate. What stage of the policy process is this?
   a. policy formation
   b. agenda setting
   c. policy adoption
   d. problem recognition and definition

2) All public issues that are viewed as requiring governmental attention are referred to as the
   a. systemic agenda.
   b. governmental agenda.
   c. institutional agenda.
   d. defining agenda.

3) The crafting of appropriate and acceptable proposed courses of action to ameliorate or resolve public problems is called
   a. agenda setting.
   b. policy formulation.
   c. policy implementation.
   d. problem resolution.

4) In order for a policy to be adopted, it is usually necessary to form
   a. majority coalitions.
   b. special interest groups.
   c. an iron triangle.
   d. authoritative panel to recommend alternatives for adoption.

5) Providing people with information, education, resources, and training as a technique of policy implementation is called a(n) _____ technique.
   a. hortatory
   b. incentive
   c. capacity
   d. authoritative

6) The process of determining whether a course of action is achieving its intended goals is called
   a. policy evaluation.
   b. problem recognition.
   c. policy implementation.
   d. policy adoption.

7) Unemployment insurance is funded through a
   a. payroll tax collected from individuals.
   b. payroll tax collected from employers.
   c. general revenue funds.
   d. state tax on employers.

8) Social insurance programs that provide cash assistance to qualified beneficiaries regardless of their income or means are called

   a. security assistance programs.
   b. grant-in-aid programs.
   c. nonmeans-based programs.
   d. means-based programs.

9) The poverty line for an urban family of four in 2003 was _____ per year.
   a. $8,990
   b. $18,810
   c. $27,649
   d. $36,136

10) Most regulatory programs established through the 1950s fell into the category of
    a.   economic regulation.
    b.   social regulation.
    c.   fiscal policy.
    d.   domestic regulation.

11) Deregulation was first made a focal point of policy making during the administration of President
    a.   Franklin Roosevelt.
    b.   Lyndon Johnson.
    c.   Gerald Ford.
    d.   George Bush.

12) Typical tools the government uses to influence the economy include
    a.   monetary policy.
    b.   fiscal policy.
    c.   social policy.
    d.   Both "a" and "b."

13) The responsibility for the formation and implementation of monetary policy thorough is ability to control the credit-creating and lending activities of the nation's banks is the
    a.   Federal Deposit Insurance Commission.
    b.   U.S. Congress.
    c.   Federal Reserve Board.
    d.   Securities and Exchange Commission.

14) The deliberate use of the national government's taxing and spending policies to influence the overall operation of the economy and maintain economics stability is called
    a.   economic policy.
    b.   fiscal policy.
    c.   monetary policy.
    d.   supply-side economic policy.

15) The idea that government spending could offset a decline in private spending and thus help maintain high levels of spending, production, and employment was advocated by
    a.   David Ricardo.
    b.   John Maynard Keynes.
    c.   Herbert Hoover.
    d.   Adam Smith.

TRUE/FALSE QUESTIONS

1) The national government has provided at least some form of health care for some citizens since 1798.

2) Eligible individuals are entitled to Social Security benefits regardless of how much unearned income they receive in addition to their Social Security benefits.

3) The initial federal food stamp program was primarily an effort to expand domestic markets for farm commodities.

4) Despite the fact that the United States spends more per person on health care than any other country, the U.S. is ranked only thirty-seventh in quality of health care, according to a World Health Organization analysis.

5) Medicare provides long-term nursing home care to all who qualify.

6) The Progressive Movement sought to bring corporate power under the control of the government and to make it more responsive to democratic control.

7) The Wagner Act increased the power of labor unions to protect workers in the United States.

8) The Fair Labor Standards Act of 1938 was intended to protect business owners from frivolous strikes by unions.

9) Congress based the passage of its social regulatory programs of the mid-1960s through mid-1970s on its commerce clause authority.

10) Due to the extensive corporate collapses due to fraud and greed in the past few years, the Bush administration has reinstituted a number of strenuous regulatory controls on business to protect consumers and stock-holders.

COMPARE AND CONTRAST

the phases of policy formation: problem recognition, agenda setting, formulation, policy adoption, budgeting, policy implementation, policy evaluation

systemic agenda and government agenda

means-tested and nonmeans-tested programs

entitlement programs and regular budget items

Medicare and Medicaid

economic regulation, social regulation, and deregulation

recession and depression

monetary and fiscal policies

ESSAY AND SHORT ANSWER QUESTIONS

1) What are public policy and social welfare policy?

2) What is considered a policy problem, and how would it be identified?

3) Fully explain the stages of the policy process.

4) What are the techniques of policy implementation? Discuss how each one works, using examples.

5) Discuss policies designed to increase income security.

6) What policies has the U.S. followed regarding health care? Which ones have been enacted, and which ones have been defeated, and why?

7) Explain the process that America went through in its evolution from a *laissez-faire* state to an interventionist state.

8) Discuss the nature of economic and social regulation in the nineteenth and twentieth centuries.

9) How does the government use fiscal and monetary policy to stabilize the economy?

10) Briefly explain the Federal Reserve System.

ANSWERS TO STUDY EXERCISES

multiple choice answers

1.	d	p. 480
2.	a	p. 480
3.	b	p. 481
4.	a	p. 484
5.	c	p. 486

6.	a	p. 487
7.	b	p. 489
8.	c	p. 490
9.	b	p. 490
10.	a	p. 505
11.	c	p. 507
12.	d	p. 509
13	c	p. 510
14.	b	p. 511
15.	b	p. 511

true/false answers

1.	T	p. 490
2.	T	p. 491
3.	T	p. 498
4.	T	p. 499
5.	F	p. 501
6.	T	p. 503
7.	T	p. 504
8.	F	p. 504
9.	T	p. 505
10.	F	p. 509

CHAPTER 14
FOREIGN AND DEFENSE POLICY

Chapter Goals and Learning Objectives

President George W. Bush in his 2005 inaugural address boldly told the world, "All who live in tyranny and hopelessness can know the United States will not ignore your oppression or excuse your oppressors. When you stand for your liberty, we will stand with you." This pledge made at the start of his second term as president indicated his willingness to further commit American strength across the planet. When he made this pledge in January of 2005, some 140,000 U.S. troops were stationed in Iraq. Some 1,400 U.S. military personnel had been killed in Iraq since the U.S. invaded that Middle Eastern country in the spring of 2003, with nearly 10,400 wounded.

The Bush Doctrine of using America's preeminent military power in preemptive attack reflects, in part, this country's status as the sole world superpower. In many ways, the United States, particularly under George W. Bush, has taken the position of using its power in directing and influencing political affairs across the globe, enforced by a military budget greater than all the major world powers combined. It is a post-Cold War policy that has developed for a number of reasons.

Americans who grew up during the height of the Cold War lived under the threat of nuclear annihilation every day. They understood that the Soviet Union had enough nuclear weapons to destroy the United States many times over. And Americans understood that we could destroy all life in the U.S.S.R. several times over as well. Americans lived "eyeball-to-eyeball" with the Soviets in a game of nuclear chicken for decades, holding each other's entire populations as hostages in a mad game called "mutually assured destruction" or MAD.

When the Cold War came to an end in 1991 after over four decades of constant, non-belligerent conflict between the U.S. and U.S.S.R., the foreign and military policy of the United States suddenly, stunningly, and completely changed. For years it was us vs. them, two gigantic titans in the ring struggling for world domination. Yet in a matter of weeks, only one titan remained standing. The United States found itself as the world's remaining superpower with a new and ill-defined mission in the world. Foreign and military policy had to undergo drastic introspection and changes. Many Americans put foreign and military affairs on a back-burner and turned to domestic matters—butter rather than guns.

Until September 11, 2001, when Americans found themselves confronting the rest of the world following the first attack on the American mainland by foreign forces since the War of 1812 (an important distinction from Pearl Harbor, which was U.S. territory, but effectively a colony). America took stock of its foreign and military policy in a new and chilling light. Afghanistan, international terrorism, Iraq, an "axis of evil" and a new concern for our place in the world became apparent to a new generation of Americans.

While most Americans pay scant attention to foreign policy except in times of crisis, our lives are intertwined as citizens of this nation with our policies in dealing with the world. We do a substantial amount of foreign trade, we have a substantial military force and substantial military commitments overseas, and we are interdependent on other economies in the world for our prosperity. Since the main purpose of government is to protect us and maintain our prosperity, it is incumbent upon Americans to understand and involve ourselves in our commitments and policies with the rest of the world.

This chapter is designed to give you a basic overview of U.S. foreign and military policy. The main topic headings of the chapter are:

- The Roots of Current U.S. Foreign and Defense Policy
- The Executive Branch and Foreign and Defense Policy Making
- Other Shapers and Influencers of Foreign and Defense Policy
- The Challenge of Balancing Foreign and Domestic Affairs

In each section, there are certain facts and ideas that you should strive to understand. Many are in boldface type and appear in both the narrative and in the glossary at the end of the book. Other ideas, dates, facts, events, people, etc. are more difficult to pull out of the narrative. (Keep in mind that studying for objective-style tests [multiple choice, T/F] is different than studying for essay tests. See the Study Guide section on test taking for hints on study skills.)

In general, after you finish reading and studying this chapter, you should understand the following:

- The roots of U.S. foreign and defense policy since it became a world power
- How the executive branch determines foreign and defense policy
- Groups that shape and influence foreign policy
- Challenges in the twenty-first century of balancing foreign and domestic affairs

Chapter Outline and Key Points

In this section, you are provided with a basic outline of the chapter and key words/points you should know. Use this outline to develop a complete outline of the material. Write the definitions or further explanations for the terms. Use the space provided in this workbook or rewrite that material in your notebook. This will help you study and remember the material in preparation for your tests, assignments, and papers.

isolationism—

unilateralism—

moralism—

pragmatism—

The Roots of Current U.S. Foreign and Defense Policy

containing the Soviet Union in the early 1960s—

Kennedy and Khrushchev in Vienna, 1961—

Cuban Missile Crisis—

partial nuclear test ban treaty—

"hot line"—

Vietnam War—

U.S. optimism wanes by end of 1960s—

Détente, Human Rights, and Renewed Containment: 1969-1981

détente—

Nixon Doctrine—

arms control agreements—

human rights—

Iranian hostage crisis—

Soviet Union invasion of Afghanistan—

Carter Doctrine—

Containment Revisited and Renewed: 1981-1989

Reagan arms build-up—

"Star Wars"—

superpower relations in 1983—

NATO—

improvements in 1984—

Reagan Doctrine—

Mikhail Gorbachev—

Searching for a New International Order: 1989-2001

Gorbachev response to revolts in Eastern Europe—

collapse of "Iron Curtain"—

Tiananmen Square, June 1989—

Operation Desert Storm—

1991 attempted Moscow coup—

collapse of Soviet Union—

post-Cold War questions—

Clinton's foreign policy agenda—

engagement—

enlargement—

North American Free Trade Agreement (NAFTA)—

World Trade Organization (WTO)—

A New Order for the Twenty-First Century?

George W. Bush agenda—

1972 Anti-Ballistic Missile Treaty—

Kyoto environmental agreement—

September 11, 2001—

al-Qaeda—

invasion of Afghanistan—

war on terrorism—

weapons of mass destruction (WMDs)—

Bush plans to invade Iraq—

Hans Blix—

Tony Blair—

"coalition of the willing"—

invasion of Iraq and overthrow of Saddam Hussein—

"Mission Accomplished"—

Bush administration underestimation of postwar situation in Iraq—

Abu Ghraib prison scandal—

no WDMs found in Iraq—

The Executive Branch and Foreign and Defense Policy-Making

The Role of the President

preeminence of president in foreign and military policy—

exclusive sources of information for president—

willingness of people of listen to the president along on foreign and domestic affairs—

The Departments of State, Defense, and Homeland Security

Department of State—

Department of Defense—

Department of Homeland Security—

largest government reorganization since when?—

The Central Intelligence Agency and National Security Council

CIA—

consist of CIA community—

CIA post September 11—

George Tenet—

NSC—

special assistant to president for national security affairs—

Other Shapers and Influencers of Foreign and Defense Policy

Congress

powers given by Congress—

how does Congress influence foreign and defense policy—

oversight powers of Congress—

Vietnam War and War Powers Act of 1973—

treaties and executive agreements—

Senate power to approve or reject treaties—

Senate has rejected treaties how many times?—

executive agreements—

appropriations power—

Congress, Reagan and funding for Contras—

The Military Industrial Complex

Eisenhower's farewell address of 1961—

military-industrial complex—

ways in which the military-industrial complex acquires power:

        1)

        2)

        3)

        4)

        5)

The News Media

reporting and investigation—

presidents' criticism of news media—

the press in Gulf War—

military uses news media for its own ends—

media coverage of Abu Ghraib prison abuses—

agenda setting—

which issues get attention, which issues do not—

influencing public opinion—

effect of media coverage of Vietnam—

news media used to build public support for war—

The Public

most Americans far more interested in domestic affairs than foreign and defense policy (Figure 14.1)—

militarism/nonmilitarism and isolationism/internationalism—

rise in presidential popularity in foreign/military crisis—

activists influence on NGOs—

The Challenge of Balancing Foreign and Domestic Affairs

grand strategy—

three elements of building a grand strategy:

1)

2)

3)

Research Ideas and Possible Paper Topics

1) Choose a foreign policy crisis (either contemporary or historical). Conduct research to determine what issues were at hand, what actors were making the decisions, and what the outcome was. Did public opinion matter? Was the president the strongest actor in the crisis? How did the various interests play themselves out?

2) American news, be it press or broadcast media, tends to skimp on international news. The argument is that Americans are not interested. Is that true? Interest increased after 9/11 but some say Americans have again lost interest in foreign news. Find public opinion polling data, ask friends and colleagues, etc. about their interest in international relations. Next, test the hypothesis that the media ignores foreign affairs. Watch several different types of media (network TV, newspapers, cable TV, news magazines) and determine if that is true. Now that you know more about U.S. foreign policy, are you more interested in such news? Discuss these issues or structure a debate about them.

3) As a class, discuss what the grand strategy of the U.S. ought to be now that some fifteen years have passed since the Cold War ended. What are U.S. national interests? Should we intervene in other country's affairs as President Bush has suggested in his second inaugural, and why or why not? What about Iraq and the Middle East? What is our national interest in that region? Trade and aid policy—with whom should we trade and to whom should we give aid? Are there limits to U.S. generosity? What are they?

4) Research the history and development of international terrorism. Has there been attacks on U.S. interests before the 9/11 attack on New York and Washington? What was U.S. policy toward international terrorism before 9/11 and after? What has happened since 9/11? Has there been any significant terrorist threats to the U.S. since 9/11? Why or why not? What is the future of U.S. anti-terrorism on the domestically and internationally?

5) Do some research on businesses in your area that are involved in international trade. Use the Internet or library to find out what kinds of businesses are doing business where and why. Are there more international ties in your area than you

thought? What kinds of impacts does this trade have on you, your town/city, the country?

Web Sites

Cryptome.com is a private Web site sponsored by private donations that honors the sacrifice of the U.S. military in Iraq. The Web site tabulates U.S. war dead and wounded in Iraq, presents the names of U.S. service men and woman killed and injured, offers links to pictures and stories about the men and women of the U.S. military who have served in Iraq, and offers links to information about the war not usually available from the government or mainstream media.

http://cryptome.org

Official site of the United States **Department of State**

http://www.state.gov

The **U.S. State Department** maintains at electronic archive of foreign policy history including documents and photographs that can be searched and accessed online.

www.state.gov/www/about_state/history/frus.html

Official Web site of the **Department of Defense**

www.dod.gov

Official Web site of the **Department of Homeland Security**

www.dhs.gov

Official Web site of the **Central Intelligence Agency**

www.cia.gov

Official Web site of the **Senate Foreign Relations Committee**

http://foreign.senate.gov

Official site of the **Pentagon**

www.defenselink.mil/pubs/pentagon

Official site of the **Air Force**

www.af.mil

Official site of the **Marine Corps**

www.hqmc.usmc.mil

Official site of the **Army**

www.army.mil

Official site of the **Navy**

www.ncts.navy.mil

Official site of the **Joint Chiefs of Staff**
www.dtic.mil/jcs

National Center for Policy Analysis is a nonprofit public policy research institute from a conservative perspective.
www.ncpa.org

Center for Defense Information is a nonprofit public policy center with a moderate to liberal perspective. "Founded in 1972 as an independent monitor of the military, the Center for Defense Information is a private, nongovernmental, research organization. Its directors and staff believe that strong social, economic, political, and military components and a healthy environment contribute equally to the nation's security. CDI seeks realistic and cost-effective military spending without excess expenditures for weapons and policies that increase the danger of war. CDI supports adequate defense by evaluating our defense needs and how best to meet them without wasteful spending or compromising our national security."
www.cdi.org

Foreign Policy in Focus is a nonprofit foreign policy study group that examines such issues from a progressive perspective.
www.fpif.org

Foreign Affairs Magazine is a monthly journal published by the Council on Foreign Relations and has long been considered one of the most prestigious publications on the issue of foreign policy. A selection of articles is online from the current issue.
www.foreignaffairs.org

The **Council on Foreign Relations**, founded in 1921, is an independent, national membership organization and a nonpartisan center for scholars dedicated to producing and disseminating ideas on U.S. foreign relation. Its Web site offers a broad range of information, data, papers and links.
www.cfr.org/index.php

Cold War Hot Links is a Web site maintained by a professor at St. Martin's College in Washington State. This site offers links to a myriad of sites dealing with the Cold War and U.S. foreign and military policy during that period following the end of WWII until 1991.
www.stmartin.edu/~dprice/cold.war.html

The Web site for the **Technical Support Work Group**, a multi-agency federal governmental study group, follows U.S. anti-terrorism developments.
www.tswg.gov

The **Office of Trade and Economic Analysis** does research and analysis of international trade issues and publishes data and statistics, which are available at this site to the public. www.ita.doc.gov/td/industry/otea

---

Practice Tests

MULTIPLE CHOICE QUESTIONS

1) A 1962 confrontation between the Soviet Union and the United States nearly escalated into nuclear war over the deployment of Soviet medium-range nuclear ballistic missiles in what country?
   a. Panama
   b. Vietnam
   c. Korea
   d. Cuba

2) In the 1960s and early 1970s, the United States military involvement in what country cost the lives of more than 58,000 American men and women?
   a. Panama
   b. Vietnam
   c. Korea
   d. Cuba

3) During the late 1970s, the relaxation of tensions between the Soviet Union and the United States was called
   a. a thaw.
   b. a respite.
   c. détente.
   d. containment.

4) The policy that the United States would provide arms and military equipment to countries but not do the fighting for them was called the _____ Doctrine.
   a. Carter
   b. Brezhnev
   c. Ford
   d. Nixon

5) The first peacetime military treaty the United States joined, this regional political and military organization was created in 1950.
   a. the UN
   b. NAFTA
   c. NATO
   d. SEATO

6) The dramatic relaxation of tensions between the United States and the Soviet Union and the decision to not subdue rebellions in Eastern Europe in 1989 came under the leadership of
   a. Nikita Khrushchev.
   b. Mikhail Gorbachev.
   c. Boris Yeltsen.
   d. Vladimir Putin.

7) The Chinese government in June 1989 crushed a student-led demonstrations for democratic reform, killing hundreds or thousands of demonstrators in the strongest anti-government protest in China since the 1949 revolution. Many students confronted Chinese tanks and troops in this location, which became synonymous with the protest.
   a. Tiananmen Square
   b. Hong Kong
   c. Taiwan
   d. the Great Wall of China

8) The policy implemented during the Clinton administration that the United States would remain actively involved in foreign affairs was known as
   a. containment.
   b. involvement.
   c. engagement.
   d. enhancement.

9) President Bush, during his first few months as president, met twice with the president of Russia,
   a. Mikhail Gorbachev.
   b. Nikita Khrushchev.
   c. Boris Yeltsin.
   d. Vladimir Putin.

10) In the early months of his administration, President Bush announced that he the United States would not abide by its signed pledge of support for an international environmental agreement known as
   a. the Moscow agreement.
   b. the Kyoto agreement.
   c. the Paris accords.
   d. NAFTA.

11) Other than Great Britain, very few major world powers agreed to invade Iraq with President Bush in 2003 without evidence that Saddam Hussein possessed or was developing weapons of mass destruction. Bush called the group of small countries that did support his invasion of Iraq
   a. the few, the proud, the invaders.
   b. the coalition of the willing.

216

c.   the magnificent seven.

d.   the axis of allies.

12)   Which branch of government plays the most important role in creating and
       implementing U.S. foreign and defense policy?
       a.   legislative
       b.   executive
       c.   judicial
       d.   adjudicative

13)   One of the significant foreign policy advantages the president has over
       Congress is
       a.   the power to declare war.
       b.   greater access to and control over information.
       c.   treaty power.
       d.   All of the above.

14)   The president has the power to make treaties
       a.   unilaterally.
       b.   with the consent of the House.
       c.   with the consent of the Senate.
       d.   with the consent of both houses of Congress.

15)   A U.S. government accord with foreign nations not requiring Senate approval is
       called a(n)
       a.   executive order.
       b.   treaty.
       c.   tariff.
       d.   executive agreement.

TRUE/FALSE QUESTIONS

1)   Richard M. Nixon was president of the United States during the Cuban
      Missile Crisis.

2)   Jimmy Carter dramatically decreased military funding and enhanced relations
      with the Soviet Union as a result of the Soviet invasion of Afghanistan.

3)   In 1983, the United States inadvertently destroyed a Korean airliner that flew into
      restricted airspace, triggering an international incident.

4)   Mikhail Gorbachev was the Soviet leader whose policies lead to a peaceful and
      unexpected breakup of the Soviet Union.

5) In the early 1990s, the U.S. and other countries immediately intervened to stop Serbia's ethnic cleansing campaign against Bosnian Muslims in the former Czechoslovakia.

6) The president is preeminent in foreign and military policy making.

7) In response to the 9/11 attacks on the United States, President Bush created the Central Intelligence Agency.

8) Congress rarely plays a significant role in foreign policy.

9) John F. Kennedy warned against a military-industrial complex in his 1961 inaugural address.

10) Public opinion polls show that most Americans are more interested in domestic affairs than foreign and defense policy.

COMPARE AND CONTRAST

treaty and executive agreement

isolationism and interventionism

unilateralism and multilateralism

Cold War, containment, NATO, and post-Cold War policy

National Security Council, National Economic Council, and the Central Intelligence Agency

Department of State, Defense and Homeland Security

American interventionism and Bush policy of preventive war

presidential vs. congressional powers in foreign affairs

media and public role in foreign policy

ESSAY AND SHORT ANSWER QUESTIONS

1) What were the views of the Framers on foreign affairs?

2) What is an executive agreement, and why is it important?

3) What is isolationism? When and why did the U.S. adopt this policy?

4) Discuss the Nixon and Carter doctrines and how did they differ?

5) Discuss the defense and foreign policies of the Reagan administration.

6) Discuss difference between the early months of the George W. Bush administration and after 9/11 with regard to foreign and military policy.

7) Discuss the importance of Mikhail Gorbachev in ending the Cold War.

8) Discuss the role of the executive branch in foreign policy making.

9) Discuss executive-legislative conflict in the realm of foreign and defense policies. What other actors also vie for influence in these decisions, and how effective are they?

10) Discuss President George W. Bush's initial rationale for the U.S. invasion of Iraq in 2003. What errors were made or falsehoods told to lead the U.S. into invading Iraq? What purpose has the war there served?

ANSWERS TO STUDY EXERCISES

multiple choice answers

1.	d	p. 517
2.	b	p. 517
3.	c	p. 518
4.	d	p. 519
5.	c	p. 520
6.	b	p. 520, 521
7.	a	p. 521
8.	c	p. 523
9.	d	p. 524
10.	b.	p. 524
11.	b	p. 528
12.	b	p. 531
13.	b	p. 533
14.	c	p. 536
15.	d	p. 536

true/false answers

1.	F	p. 516
2.	F	p. 519, 520
3.	F	p. 520
4.	T	p. 520, 521
5.	F	p. 522
6.	T	p. 532
7.	F	p. 534
8.	F	p. 535
9.	F	p. 538
10.	T	p. 539